From our Kitchen to Yours

ALL-TIME-FAVORITE RECIPES

From

ARIZONA

COOKS

Dedication

For every cook who wants to create amazing
recipes from the great state of Arizona.

Appreciation

Thanks to all our Arizona cooks who shared their
delightful and delicious recipes with us!

Gooseberry Patch
An imprint of Globe Pequot
64 South Main Street
Essex, CT 06426
www.gooseberrypatch.com
1 800 854 6673

Copyright 2024, Gooseberry Patch
978-162093-557-6

Do you have a tried & true recipe...tip, craft or
memory that you'd like to see featured in a
Gooseberry Patch cookbook? Visit our website at
www.gooseberrypatch.com and follow the easy steps
to submit your favorite family recipe.

Or send them to us at:

Gooseberry Patch
PO Box 812
Columbus, OH 43216-0812

Don't forget to include the number of servings your
recipe makes, plus your name, address, phone
number and email address. If we select your recipe,
your name will appear right along with it...and you'll
receive a FREE copy of the book!

ARIZONA COOKS

ICONIC ARIZONA

Whether you're standing on top of a red rock plateau, in a lush valley or even on "Four Corners," the state motto, "God enriches" (Ditat Deus), is a true indication of the beauty to be found in the painted landscapes and delicately carved canyons of the great state of Arizona.

Brimming with a rich history, Arizona is as wonderfully diverse as the Grand Canyon is deep. Historical events like the Hohokams village development, the discovery of gold and the expansion of trade, reflect the cultural influences from Native Americans, Mexicans, and early ranch settlers.

Arizona's colorful cuisine springs from food staples like squash, beans and corn along with lamb, cholla buds and frybread. Salsa, tamales, enchiladas and chimichangas are popular throughout the state as well as traditional "Cowboy Chow" consisting of beans, biscuits, meats, and dried fruits.

When family in Arizona gather 'round the table, it's not uncommon to find them dining on syrups, candies, jellies, salsas or barbecue sauces made with parts of the native saguaro cactus.

Inside this cookbook you will find delicious tried & true recipes from cooks all around the great state of Arizona, including Rancho Grande Casserole, Enchilada Lasagna, Creamy Green Chile Zucchini, Mrs. V's Southwest Quiche, Vagabond Chicken Bundles, Mini Wonton Salsa Baskets, Date-Nut Roll and Nutmeg Feather Cake. Enjoy!

OUR STORY

Back in 1984, our families were neighbors in little Delaware, Ohio. With small children, we wanted to do what we loved and stay home with the kids too. We had always shared a love of home cooking and so, **Gooseberry Patch** was born.

Almost immediately, we found a connection with our customers and it wasn't long before these friends started sharing recipes. Since then we've enjoyed publishing hundreds of cookbooks with your tried & true recipes.

We know we couldn't have done it without our friends all across the country and we look forward to continuing to build a community with you. Welcome to the **Gooseberry Patch** family!

JoAnn & Vickie

TABLE OF CONTENTS

CHAPTER ONE

CACTUS BLOSSOM
Breakfasts

ENJOY THESE TASTY BREAKFAST RECIPES THAT BRING YOU TO THE TABLE WITH A HEARTY "GOOD MORNING!" AND CARRY YOU THROUGH THE DAY TO TACKLE WHATEVER COMES YOUR WAY.

BREAKFAST BURRITO ROLL-UPS

ANGELA MURPHY
TEMPE, AZ

Finger food for breakfast! Use whatever veggies you like.

3 T. green pepper, chopped
1 t. olive oil
3 eggs, beaten
1 T. water
2 8-inch whole-wheat flour tortillas
1/2 to 3/4 c. shredded Mexican-blend cheese

In a skillet, sauté green pepper in oil until tender. Remove pepper from pan. Whisk together eggs and water; add to hot skillet. Cook until set; do not stir or scramble. Flip to cook the other side. Cut in half; place half of eggs on each tortilla. Top with pepper and cheese; roll up and slice. Serve immediately.

Serves one to two.

CHOCOLATE-BANANA OVERNIGHT OATS

MARLA KINNERSLEY
SURPRISE, AZ

We love waking up to this super-delicious, healthy breakfast. We put it together the night before, then in the morning we just stir in the sliced bananas and peanut butter...and enjoy!

1 c. old-fashioned oats, uncooked and divided
1 c. unsweetened vanilla almond milk, divided
4 T. baking cocoa
4 T. honey
4 t. chia seed
1-1/3 t. vanilla extract
1 ripe banana, thinly sliced
4 T. creamy peanut butter

To each of 4 mini canning jars or cereal bowls, add 1/4 cup oats and 1/4 cup milk; stir. Divide cocoa, honey, chia seed and vanilla among jars; stir well. Cover and refrigerate overnight. In the morning, divide banana slices among jars; top evenly with peanut butter and serve.

Makes 4 servings.

CHRISTMAS SAUSAGE SOUFFLÉ

CAROL JORDAN
GILBERT, AZ

I got the basis for this recipe from my sister in Utah and have been making it for my family ever since. That was over 20 years ago! On Christmas morning, I put this in to bake and then we enjoy our time opening presents with the wonderful smell of baking breakfast.

In a large bowl, whisk together eggs, 1-1/2 cups milk, salt and pepper. Stir in sausage, bread and cheese. Cover and refrigerate overnight. In the morning, transfer mixture to a greased 13"x9" baking pan. In a separate bowl, whisk together soup and remaining milk; spoon over top. Bake, uncovered, at 350 degrees for 1-1/2 hours, or until set.

Makes 15 servings.

10 eggs, beaten
1-1/2 c. plus 2/3 c. milk, divided
salt and pepper to taste
2 c. ground pork breakfast sausage, browned and drained
20 slices white bread, torn into small pieces
2-1/2 c. shredded Cheddar cheese
10-3/4 oz. can cream of mushroom soup

KITCHEN TIP

Spray measuring cups with non-stick spray before filling them with sticky ingredients like peanut butter for easy removal.

GEN'S SHRIMP CREOLE

GEN CORNISH
ARIZONA CITY, AZ

This is such a delicious, quick-to-make recipe. For an elegant holiday breakfast or brunch, I serve it spooned over egg omelets. I like to make a couple batches and freeze them in pint containers.

1/2 c. green pepper, chopped
1/2 c. onion, chopped
2 T. butter
14-1/2 oz. can stewed tomatoes
1/2 t. sugar
1/2 t. chili powder
1/8 t. garlic powder
1/8 t. dried thyme
1/16 t. cayenne pepper
1/2 bay leaf
salt and pepper to taste
20 to 30 frozen uncooked shrimp, cleaned and thawed
cooked rice

In a skillet over medium heat, sauté pepper and onion in butter until crisp-tender. Add tomatoes with juice and seasonings. Reduce heat to medium-low; simmer for 20 minutes. Add shrimp and cook until no longer transparent, about 3 to 4 minutes. Discard bay leaf. Serve over cooked rice.

Makes 4 servings.

CHOCOLATE GRAVY & CRESCENTS

SHERRY SHEEHAN
PHOENIX, AZ

My brother makes a similar recipe for breakfast every year on the day after Thanksgiving. I never could get him to share his exact recipe, so I made up this recipe based on the taste and a couple secrets that I knew he used. I think it is pretty close. It is a wonderful breakfast for special occasions. The gravy can be served over biscuits, but I enjoy the richness that the crescent rolls give it. We always serve crispy bacon alongside this dish.

Bake crescent rolls according to package directions; cool. Meanwhile, melt butter in a saucepan over medium heat. Add flour, cocoa and sugar; whisk together until smooth. Add milk to saucepan; continue whisking until smooth. Cook for 2 minutes, or until thickened and smooth. Add a little more milk if gravy becomes thicker than desired. Remove from heat; stir in vanilla and salt. Serve chocolate gravy ladled over warm crescent rolls.

8-oz. tube refrigerated crescent rolls
5 T. butter, sliced
3 T. all-purpose flour
3 T. dark baking cocoa
1/4 c. sugar
1-1/4 c. milk
1-1/2 t. vanilla extract
1/4 t. salt

Serves 4.

JUST FOR FUN

Twenty-two federally recognized Native American tribes call Arizona home.

ALL-TIME-FAVORITE RECIPES FROM ARIZONA COOKS **11**

SAVORY SPINACH SOUFFLÉ

ANGELA MURPHY
TEMPE, AZ

*A tasty spinach soufflé, paired with a glass of orange juice and a hot mug
of coffee, will make any morning bright. Try using Swiss cheese instead of
Cheddar for something deliciously different.*

**2 16-oz. pkgs. frozen
spinach, thawed and
well drained**

1/4 c. onion, grated

**8-oz. pkg. low-fat cream
cheese, softened**

1/2 c. mayonnaise

**1/2 c. shredded Cheddar
cheese**

2 eggs, beaten

1/4 t. pepper

1/8 t. nutmeg

In a bowl, mix together spinach and onion; set
aside. In a separate bowl, beat together remaining
ingredients until well blended; fold into spinach
mixture. Spoon into a lightly greased slow cooker.
Cover and cook on high setting for 2 to 3 hours, until
set.

Serves 4 to 6.

HOLIDAY SAUSAGE RING

GEN CORNISH
ARIZONA CITY, AZ

*We traditionally host Christmas brunch at our house. Everyone
always expects to see this sausage ring on the table loaded with
fluffy scrambled eggs in the center. It's definitely a family favorite!*

**2 lbs. ground pork
sausage**

**1-1/2 c. dry bread
crumbs**

2 eggs, beaten

**1/4 c. fresh parsley,
chopped**

2 T. onion, grated

Lightly grease a 9" ring mold. In a large bowl,
combine all ingredients; mix well. Pack into mold.
Bake, uncovered, at 350 degrees for 20 minutes.
Remove from oven; drain. Return to oven; bake
20 minutes longer. Turn out onto a warm platter.

Serves 8 to 10.

CRUNCHY VEGGIE CREAM CHEESE & BAGELS

MARLA KINNERSLEY
SURRISE, AZ

I have always loved going out for bagels in the morning and have enjoyed toasted bagels with veggie cream cheese. I finally decided to just make my own! This is delicious, nutritious and doesn't last long at our house.

In a large bowl, combine all ingredients except bagels. Blend well. Spread generously on toasted bagels.

Makes 8 servings.

2 8-oz. pkgs. light cream cheese, room temperature

1 carrot, peeled and grated

1/2 red pepper, grated

1 stalk celery, grated

4 radishes, peeled and grated

3 green onions, finely chopped

1/8 t. salt

2 t. pepper

8 wheat bagels, split and toasted

JUST FOR FUN

Tucson is sometimes called the astronomy capital of the world (telescopes are on Kitt Peak, Mount Hopkins, and Mount Graham).

MY MOM'S MUFFIN DOUGHNUTS

LAURA PARKER
FLAGSTAFF, AZ

My mom made these often! It was always fun to find them stacked on a plate. I still enjoy making them for my adult daughters.

2 c. all-purpose flour
1/2 t. salt
1 T. baking powder
1/2 t. nutmeg
1/2 c. plus 1/2 t. margarine, divided
1-1/2 c. sugar, divided
1 egg, beaten
3/4 c. milk
3/4 c. semi-sweet chocolate chips
1/2 c. chopped pecans
2 t. cinnamon

Combine flour, salt, baking powder, nutmeg, 1/2 teaspoon margarine, 1/2 cup sugar, egg and milk. Fold in chocolate chips and pecans. Fill greased muffin cups 2/3 full. Bake at 350 degrees for 20 minutes. Remove immediately from pan. Melt the remaining margarine; roll muffins in margarine. Combine remaining sugar and cinnamon; roll muffins in mixture.

Makes one dozen.

SOUR CREAM COFFEE CAKE

EMILY SALSKY
TEMPE, AZ

My mother makes this coffee cake every Christmas morning. When my siblings and I were younger, it would always be baking when we came downstairs to open presents. Now that we're older, she still makes it but not as early! The scent of this cake will always bring back fond memories. I look forward to making it for my own children someday.

In a bowl, combine flour, baking powder, baking soda, sugar, salt, butter, eggs and sour cream. In a separate bowl, combine brown sugar, cinnamon and nuts. Pour half the batter into a greased tube or Bundt® pan; sprinkle with half the brown sugar mixture. Repeat layers once. Bake at 350 degrees for 35 to 45 minutes, until cake tests clean with a skewer.

Serves 12.

1-3/4 c. all-purpose flour
1 t. baking powder
1 t. baking soda
1 c. sugar
1/4 t. salt
1-1/2 c. butter, softened
2 eggs, beaten
1 c. sour cream
3/4 c. brown sugar, packed
1 T. cinnamon
3/4 c. chopped nuts

MRS. V'S SOUTHWEST QUICHE

JAMIE VOLNER
TUCSON, AZ

I have to admit I am very picky about my quiche. So, many moons ago, not even knowing how to make a quiche, I practiced, flopped and failed until I created this one. It became an instant hit with the family!

9-inch deep-dish pie crust

8 slices bacon, chopped

4 green onions, chopped

1 c. shredded Swiss cheese, divided

1 c. shredded Pepper Jack cheese, divided

6 eggs

1 c. whipping cream

1/2 t. salt

1/8 t. white pepper

1/8 t. cayenne pepper

1/2 t. nutmeg

Place crust in a 9" pie plate; pierce bottom and sides of crust several times with a fork. Bake at 400 degrees for 5 minutes. Remove from oven and set aside. Cook bacon in a skillet over medium heat until crisp; drain on paper towels. Combine bacon, onions and half of cheeses in crust. In a bowl, beat together eggs, cream and seasonings. Pour over mixture in crust. Sprinkle with remaining cheeses and nutmeg. Bake at 350 degrees for 50 minutes to one hour, until a toothpick inserted in the center tests clean. If edge of crust browns too quickly, cover with strips of aluminum foil. Let cool 10 minutes before slicing. Cut into wedges to serve.

Serves 6.

BACON-WRAPPED EGG CUPS

MARY GARCIA
PHOENIX, AZ

These tasty little breakfast cups are a hit at breakfast time. We serve them on top of thick toast slices with a few sprinkles of hot sauce or catsup.

Cook bacon in a skillet over medium heat until almost crisp; drain on paper towels. Scramble eggs to desired doneness in drippings in skillet; set aside. In a bowl, combine vegetables and garlic; season with salt and pepper. Lightly grease 6 small ramekins or custard dishes. Arrange one slice of bacon around the inside of each ramekin. Evenly spoon egg mixture and vegetables into ramekins. Place a trivet in a slow cooker; put ramekins on trivet. Add water to slow cooker to a depth of about one inch. Cover and cook on high setting for 1-1/2 to 2 hours, until warmed through and vegetables are tender.

6 slices thick-cut
   peppered bacon
6 eggs
1 c. sliced mushrooms
3 roma tomatoes, diced
1 green pepper, diced
1 t. garlic, minced
salt and pepper to taste

Serves 6.

FAMILY-TIME CONVERSATION

Arizona observes Mountain Standard Time on a year round basis. The one exception is the Navajo Nation, located in the northeast corner of the state, which observes the daylight savings time change.

COZY BREAKFAST CASSEROLE

PATTY HINER
NEW RIVER, AZ

This is our favorite weekend breakfast & brunch meal. If you prefer, use browned ground pork sausage instead of links...even add diced onions and green peppers.

- 3 lbs. potatoes, peeled and cubed
- 2 T. oil
- salt and pepper to taste
- 1 lb. bacon, crisply cooked and crumbled
- 1 lb. smoked pork sausage links, browned and cut into bite-size pieces
- 1/2 lb. cooked ham, cubed
- 2 c. shredded Cheddar cheese

In a large skillet over medium heat, cook potatoes in oil until golden. Season with salt and pepper. Add remaining ingredients except cheese; reduce heat. Cover and cook for about 15 minutes, or until potatoes are tender, stirring occasionally. Transfer to a greased 13"x9" baking pan. Add cheese and mix. Bake, uncovered, at 350 degrees for 10 minutes, or until cheese is melted.

Serves 8 to 10.

MEXICAN BREAKFAST BAKE

EVA MORGAN
CHINO VALLEY, AZ

We make this for breakfast whenever we're camping.

- 3/4 lb. ground pork sausage
- 1 doz. eggs, beaten
- 4-oz. can green chiles, drained
- 4-oz. can sliced mushrooms, drained
- 1 onion, chopped
- 1 loaf French bread
- 8-oz. pkg. shredded Mexican-blend cheese

Brown sausage in a large skillet over medium heat; drain. Add eggs, chiles, mushrooms and onion. Lower heat and cook until eggs are set. Slice bread in half horizontally; hollow out both halves, reserving removed bread for another use. Sprinkle cheese in bottom half of bread. Spoon egg mixture into bread; top with remaining bread half. Wrap in aluminum foil; heat through on the camp fire.

Serves 6.

HAPPY APPLE PANCAKES

**KATHY MURRAY-STRUNK
CHANDLER, AZ**

I developed this from a basic pancake recipe I've had for years. I call it Happy Apple Pancakes because my family is really happy when I make them! I came up with the syrup recipe one Saturday morning when I was low on maple syrup...it's delicious too.

In a bowl, beat eggs with an electric mixer on medium speed until fluffy. Stir in remaining ingredients just until smooth. Pour batter onto a hot griddle over medium-high heat by 1/4 cupfuls. Cook until pancakes are puffed and dry around the edges. Turn and cook other side until golden. Drizzle pancakes with Cream & Sugar Syrup and serve.

Makes 16 pancakes.

Cream & Sugar Syrup:
In a saucepan over low heat, melt butter with half-and-half just until starting to bubble. Add brown sugar; stir until completely smooth. Stir in vanilla.

2 eggs
2 c. all-purpose flour
1 c. half-and-half
1 c. Granny Smith applesauce
1/4 c. extra-light olive oil
3 T. sugar
2 T. baking powder
1 t. salt
3/4 t. cinnamon
1/4 t. allspice

CREAM & SUGAR SYRUP
1-1/2 T. butter, sliced
1-1/4 c. brown sugar, packed
1/4 c. half-and-half
1/4 t. vanilla extract

STUFFED FRENCH TOAST LOGS

SYLVIA STACHURA
MESA, AZ

These delicious cinnamon treats can be prepared ahead of time and refrigerated. In the morning, simply bake and watch the smiles!

24 slices white sandwich bread, crusts removed

2 8-oz. pkgs. cream cheese, softened

2 egg yolks

1-3/4 c. sugar, divided

1-1/2 c. butter, melted

4 t. cinnamon

Garnish: maple syrup, whipped cream

Flatten bread slices with a rolling pin; set aside. In a bowl, beat together cream cheese, egg yolks and 1/2 cup sugar. Spread mixture evenly on bread slices; roll up, jelly-roll style. Place melted butter in a shallow bowl. Combine cinnamon and remaining sugar in a separate shallow bowl. Lightly dip rolls in butter, then in cinnamon-sugar. Place on ungreased baking sheets. Bake at 350 degrees for 20 minutes, or until golden. Serve topped with maple syrup and whipped cream.

Makes about 6 servings.

CHEESY SAUSAGE-MUFFIN BAKE

KAREN DAVIS
GLENDALE, AZ

Easy to put together for breakfast meetings at work, tailgating, you name it! Sometimes I'll spice it up with Pepper Jack cheese.

1/2 lb. ground pork breakfast sausage

8 English muffins, cut into 6 pieces, divided

1-1/2 c. shredded Cheddar cheese, divided

5 eggs, beaten

1-1/4 c. milk

1-1/2 t. salt

1/2 t. pepper

Brown sausage in a skillet over medium heat; drain well. Spread half of English muffin pieces evenly in a greased 8"x8" baking pan. Layer with half each of sausage and cheese. Repeat layering; set aside. In a bowl, whisk together remaining ingredients; spoon evenly on top. Cover and refrigerate for 2 hours or overnight. Uncover; bake at 325 degrees for 40 to 50 minutes, until center is set. Let cool for 5 minutes; cut into squares and serve.

Makes 4 to 6 servings.

CHEDDAR-CHILE BRUNCH POTATOES

KATHY ARNER
PHOENIX, AZ

This recipe came to me years ago from the school where I work...it is requested every time we have a staff breakfast. It's easy to make and can be made the night before. I have served it at church brunches too and there's never any leftovers. My family pouts when they know the whole pan goes with me, so I have to make two pans!

Mix all ingredients except hashbrowns in a large bowl; stir until well mixed. Add hashbrowns and stir until coated well. Transfer to a greased 15"x11" baking pan. Bake, uncovered, at 375 degrees for one hour, or until deep golden. Let stand for 5 minutes before serving.

Makes 12 servings.

- 1-lb. pkg. ground pork sausage, browned and drained
- 16-oz. container light sour cream
- 10-3/4 oz. can cream of chicken soup
- 7-oz. can diced mild green chiles
- 8-oz. pkg. shredded Cheddar cheese
- 30-oz. pkg. frozen shredded hashbrowns, thawed
- 30-oz. pkg. frozen spicy or western shredded hashbrowns, thawed

PRALINE PECAN BISCUITS

DEBRA EATON
MESA, AZ

Serve warm with honey...so good!

36 pecan halves
1/2 c. butter, sliced
1/2 c. brown sugar, packed
1 T. cinnamon
2 c. buttermilk biscuit baking mix
1/3 c. milk
1/3 c. applesauce

In each cup of a greased 12-cup muffin tin, place 3 pecan halves, 2 teaspoons butter and 2 teaspoons brown sugar. Bake at 450 degrees just until butter melts; set aside. Combine remaining ingredients in a mixing bowl, beating about 20 strokes. Spoon mixture into muffin cups. Bake for 10 minutes at 450 degrees; invert on a serving plate. Serve warm.

Makes one dozen.

GARDEN-FRESH EGG CASSEROLE

ANNE MUNS
SCOTTSDALE, AZ

Fresh tomatoes and spinach turn this breakfast casserole into something extra special. I think it's perfect for overnight guests.

1 c. buttermilk
1/2 c. onion, grated
1-1/2 c. shredded Monterey Jack cheese
1 c. cottage cheese
1 c. spinach, chopped
1 c. tomatoes, chopped
1/2 c. butter, melted
18 eggs, beaten

Mix all ingredients together; pour into a greased 13"x9" baking pan. Cover; refrigerate overnight. Bake at 350 degrees for 50 minutes to one hour.

Serves 8 to 10.

EASY EGG BAKE

MARY GARCIA
PHOENIX, AZ

I've made this dish often to share with friends. It just takes a few minutes to put together and pop in the oven! Change up the ingredients as you like...sometimes I'll omit the bacon.

Spray a 13"x9" baking pan with non-stick vegetable spray. Spread potatoes in pan. Using kitchen scissors, snip bacon into pieces over potatoes. Bake, uncovered, at 350 degrees for about 15 minutes; remove from oven. Whisk together eggs and milk; pour over baked layer. Sprinkle with salt, pepper and cheese. Return to oven, uncovered, for 25 to 30 minutes, until eggs are set and cheese is melted. Cut into squares.

Serves 8.

20-oz. pkg. refrigerated diced potatoes with onions
6-oz. pkg. precooked bacon
6 to 8 eggs, beaten
1/4 c. milk
salt and pepper to taste
8-oz. pkg. shredded sharp Cheddar cheese

BLUEBERRY-LEMON CREPES

KAREN DAVIS
GLENDALE, AZ

A scrumptious and refreshing breakfast!

Combine cream cheese, half-and-half, lemon juice and dry pudding mix in a bowl. Beat with an electric mixer on low speed for 2 minutes. Refrigerate for 30 minutes. Lightly grease a 6" skillet and place over medium-high heat. In a bowl, combine biscuit baking mix, egg and milk. Beat until smooth. Pour 2 tablespoons of batter into skillet for each crepe. Rotating the skillet quickly, allow batter to cover the bottom of the skillet. Cook each crepe until lightly golden, then flip, cooking again until just golden. Spoon 2 tablespoonfuls of cream cheese mixture onto each crepe and roll up. Top with remaining cream cheese mixture and pie filling.

Makes 6 servings.

3-oz. pkg. cream cheese, softened
1-1/2 c. half-and-half
1 T. lemon juice
3-3/4 pkg. instant lemon pudding mix
1/2 c. biscuit baking mix
1 egg
6 T. milk
1 c. blueberry pie filling

MUSHROOM & CHEESE STRATA

ANGELA MURPHY
TEMPE, AZ

A brunch favorite! I keep a bag in the freezer for extra slices of bread, then when I have enough, I treat the family.

1/2 lb. sliced mushrooms

1 T. olive oil

5 c. day-old Italian or white bread, cut into 1-inch cubes and divided

2 c. shredded Swiss cheese, divided

8 eggs

2-1/2 c. milk

2 T. fresh thyme, snipped

1 T. Dijon mustard

1/4 t. salt

pepper to taste

In a skillet over medium heat, sauté mushrooms in oil for about 5 minutes, until mushrooms are softened and liquid is evaporated. Spray a slow cooker generously with non-stick vegetable spray. Spread 1/3 of bread in slow cooker; spoon half of mushrooms over bread and top with 1/3 of cheese. Repeat layering with half of remaining bread, remaining mushrooms and half of remaining cheese. Top with remaining bread. In a large bowl, beat together eggs, milk, thyme, mustard, salt and pepper; pour over bread. Gently press down bread to absorb egg mixture. Sprinkle remaining cheese on top. Cover and cook on low setting for 7 to 8 hours. Uncover; let stand for 15 minutes before serving.

Makes 8 servings.

JUST FOR FUN

Grand Canyon's Marble Canyon got its name from its thousand-foot-thick seam of marble and for its walls eroded to a polished glass finish.

CHUCKWAGON BREAKFAST SKILLET

VICKIE
GOOSEBERRY PATCH

For a head start on this hearty, delicious breakfast, the potatoes can be cooked ahead of time.

Add potatoes to a saucepan of boiling water. Cook over medium heat for 12 to 15 minutes, until tender; drain. Meanwhile, in a large skillet over medium heat, cook bacon until crisp. Remove bacon to a paper towel; reserve some of drippings in skillet. Add potatoes and one to 2 tablespoons oil to skillet; sauté until golden. Add peppers, onion, mushrooms, salt and pepper; sauté until vegetables are tender. Drain; stir in bacon. Top with cheese; reduce heat to low. In a separate skillet over medium heat, scramble or fry eggs in butter as desired. To serve, spoon potato mixture into a large serving dish; top with eggs. Garnish, if desired.

Serves 6 to 8.

2 lbs. potatoes, peeled and cubed

1/2 lb. bacon, chopped

1 to 2 T. oil

1 green or red pepper, sliced

1 onion, sliced

2 c. sliced mushrooms

salt and pepper to taste

2 c. shredded Colby cheese

2 T. butter

8 eggs

Optional: fresh chives or parsley, chopped

MULTI-GRAIN WAFFLES

**KAREN DAVIS
GLENDALE, AZ**

A hearty waffle that gets the day off to a good start!

2 c. buttermilk
1/2 c. old-fashioned oats, uncooked
2/3 c. whole-wheat flour
2/3 c. all-purpose flour
1/4 c. toasted wheat germ
1-1/2 t. baking powder
1/2 t. baking soda
1/4 t. salt
1 t. cinnamon
2 eggs, lightly beaten
1/4 c. brown sugar, packed
1 T. canola oil
2 t. vanilla extract
Garnish: butter, maple syrup or fruit jam

In a bowl, combine buttermilk and oats; let stand for 15 minutes. In a separate bowl, whisk together flours, wheat germ, baking powder, baking soda, salt and cinnamon; set aside. Stir eggs, brown sugar, oil and vanilla into oat mixture; add to flour mixture. Stir just until moistened. Spoon batter by 1/2 to 2/3 cupfuls onto a greased hot waffle iron. Bake according to manufacturer's directions.

Makes 8 waffles.

PRESENTATION

Make cutlery easy for your guests to grab. Just take disposable napkins and individually wrap around the plasticware, then take bakers twine and tie the wrapped cutlery. You can even tie it to individual drink bottles for even more convenience!

MEXICAN GARDEN VEGETABLE OMELET

SHERRY SHEEHAN
PHOENIX, AZ

I have very fond memories of growing squash with my dad and I try to include them in a lot of recipes. I also love Tex-Mex flavors. When my doctor put me on a very low-carb diet, I started making up omelet recipes to try. This one is a real winner!

In a large non-stick skillet over medium heat, sauté vegetables in oil until tender, about 3 to 4 minutes. Remove vegetables to a plate. Beat eggs in a bowl; beat in seasonings. Pour egg mixture into skillet. Cook for about one minute, until eggs set slightly on bottom of skillet. With a non-stick spatula, push a portion of eggs toward center of skillet; allow liquid portion on top to flow outward. Repeat as needed until omelet is nearly set, about 3 to 4 minutes. Spoon vegetables onto half of the omelet. Top with 1/4 cup cheese; fold over. Sprinkle remaining cheese on top. Cook about one more minute, until cheese starts to melt. Remove to a plate; top with picante sauce.

Makes one serving.

1/4 c. zucchini, sliced and quartered

1/4 c. yellow squash, sliced and quartered

1/4 c. red pepper, diced

1 t. extra virgin olive oil

3 eggs, or 2 eggs plus 1 egg white

1/4 t. ground cumin

salt and pepper to taste

1/4 c. plus 1 T. shredded Pepper Jack cheese, divided

Garnish: 1 T. picante sauce

CHAPTER TWO

SUNSET CRATER

Salads & Sides

**TOSS TOGETHER GREAT TASTE AND
HEALTHY GOODNESS TO MAKE
FRESH, SATISFYING AND TASTY
SALADS AND SIDES THAT ARE
PACKED WITH FULL-ON FLAVOR.**

TOMATO SALAD WITH GRILLED BREAD

**BEV FISHER
MESA, AZ**

I found this unusual recipe and then tweaked it to make it my own. It's great for backyard barbecues. I guarantee you'll like it, too!

4 lbs. tomatoes, cut into chunks

2 cucumbers, peeled and sliced

4-oz. container crumbled reduced-fat feta cheese

1/4 c. balsamic vinegar

1/4 t. pepper

4 thick slices crusty whole-grain bread, cubed

1 c. watermelon, cut into 1/2-inch cubes

1 red onion, very thinly sliced and separated into rings

2 T. sliced black olives, drained

1 T. canola oil

1/4 c. fresh basil, torn

Combine tomatoes, cucumber, cheese, vinegar and pepper in a large serving bowl. Toss to mix; cover and chill one hour. Place bread cubes on an ungreased baking sheet. Bake at 350 degrees for 5 minutes, or until lightly golden. At serving time, add bread cubes and remaining ingredients to tomato mixture. Toss very lightly and serve immediately.

Serves 6.

SCALLOPED POTATOES

LYNNETTE ZAUNMILLER
SAN TAN VALLEY, AZ

*My mother used to make this recipe quite often...there were three of us
girls and we all loved it!*

In a saucepan over medium heat, cover potatoes
with water and cook until almost tender; drain.
Meanwhile, cook bacon and onion in a skillet over
medium heat. Drain, reserving 2 tablespoons
drippings. Add coating mix, salt and milk to reserved
drippings; cook until thickened. Fold potatoes into
bacon mixture. Transfer to a greased 3-1/2 quart
casserole dish and bake, covered, at 350 degrees
for 30 minutes. Remove cover, top with cheese
and bake for another 15 minutes, or until cheese is
melted.

Serves 6.

3 potatoes, peeled and
  sliced
6 slices bacon, halved
1 onion, chopped
3 T. fried chicken
  coating mix
1/2 t. salt
2 c. milk
1 c. shredded Cheddar
  cheese

DIJON-GINGER CARROTS

ANGELA MURPHY
TEMPE, AZ

*Sprinkle carrots with a little snipped fresh chives or fresh mint, tangy
mustard and ginger, sweet brown sugar...I just adore this super-
simple dressed-up carrot recipe!*

Combine all ingredients in a slow cooker; stir. Cover
and cook on high setting for 2 to 3 hours, until
carrots are tender, stirring twice during cooking.

Makes 10 to 12 servings.

12 carrots, peeled and
  sliced 1/4-inch thick
1/3 c. Dijon mustard
1/2 c. brown sugar,
  packed
1 t. fresh ginger, peeled
  and minced
1/2 t. salt
1/8 t. pepper

SKILLET FAJITA VEGETABLES

SHERRY SHEEHAN
PHOENIX, AZ

After I was put on an ultra low-carb diet, I looked for something that would give me the flavor of fajitas without the carbs from the flour tortillas. This recipe for a tasty side dish is what I came up with. Make it a delicious main dish by adding sliced grilled steak or chicken breast.

2 T. extra-virgin olive oil

1 onion, cut into small wedges

1 clove garlic, minced

1 green pepper, cut into strips

1 red pepper, cut into strips

1 orange or yellow pepper, cut into strips

1 t. ground cumin

In a large cast-iron skillet, heat oil over medium-high heat. Add onion and garlic; sauté for one to 2 minutes. Add peppers; sauté for another 5 to 6 minutes until soft, golden and caramelized, stirring occasionally. Stir in cumin; serve immediately.

Makes 6 servings.

CINNAMON APPLES

KIMBERLY MARLATT
YUMA, AZ

My one goal for Christmas Day was not to spend the whole day in the kitchen. You can make these delicious apples a couple of days in advance and just reheat them in the microwave!

2 T. butter

4 apples, peeled, cored and sliced

1/3 c. brown sugar, packed

2 T. lemon juice

3/4 t. cinnamon

In a saucepan over medium heat, melt butter. Add remaining ingredients; cook and stir until apples are golden and soft. Serve immediately, or cover and refrigerate until ready to serve.

Serves 4 to 6.

HOT & TASTY HOAGIES

KAREN DAVIS
GLENDALE, AZ

Hoagies, poorboys, grinders, submarine sandwiches...whatever you call 'em, at our house we love 'em! Use any combination of deli meats and cheeses you like.

Brush both cut sides of each roll with salad dressing. Layer bottom halves of rolls evenly with meats and cheese. Top with tomato, onion and pepperoncini, if desired. Replace tops of rolls; wrap rolls in aluminum foil. Bake at 375 degrees for 12 to 15 minutes. Carefully remove foil before serving.

Makes 6 sandwiches.

6 6-inch hoagie rolls, split

1/2 c. Italian salad dressing

1/2 lb. deli ham, sliced

1/2 lb. deli salami, sliced

1/2 lb. deli capicola, sliced

8-oz. pkg. provolone cheese slices

1 to 2 tomatoes, thinly sliced

1/2 onion, thinly sliced

Optional: pepperoncini

PRESENTATION

When hosting, tie up sandwiches with parchment paper and cooking twine for a fun and easy-to-eat presentation.

ROASTED GARDEN FLATBREADS

DARCY OBAR
GOLDEN VALLEY, AZ

I created this recipe when my mother was visiting. Even my father enjoyed it and he usually snubs meatless recipes!

2 naan flatbreads or pita rounds

3 T. olive oil, divided

1 zucchini, quartered and sliced

1 c. baby portabella mushrooms, sliced

1/2 c. marinated artichoke hearts, drained

1/4 c. sliced black olives, drained

1/4 red onion, chopped

1 t. salt

1/4 t. pepper

2 T. Italian seasoning, divided

1/2 c. cream cheese, softened

1/4 c. grated Parmesan cheese

8 slices tomato

4 slices provolone cheese

Brush flatbreads or pitas with one tablespoon oil; place on an ungreased baking sheet. Bake at 400 degrees for 5 minutes, or until lightly golden. Cool on a wire rack. Increase oven to 425 degrees. Add all vegetables except tomato to baking sheet. Sprinkle with salt, pepper and one tablespoon Italian seasoning. Drizzle lightly with remaining oil and toss to coat. Bake until vegetables start to soften, about 20 minutes. In a bowl, blend cheeses and remaining Italian seasoning; spread over cooled flatbreads. Divide roasted vegetables between flatbreads; spread to cover. Arrange tomato and cheese slices on top. Bake an additional 6 to 7 minutes, until crisp and golden.

Serves 2 to 4.

HONEY-MUSTARD SLAW

MELISSA CURRIE
PHOENIX, AZ

This zesty slaw is fantastic with any kind of barbecue...perfect for autumn tailgating!

In a bowl, mix mayonnaise, sour cream, honey and mustard. Cover and refrigerate up to one day in advance. Shortly before serving time, combine coleslaw mix and optional ingredients, if using, in a serving bowl. Add mayonnaise mixture; toss to coat. Add pecans to taste; mix again and serve immediately.

Serves 6.

1/2 c. mayonnaise
1/2 c. sour cream
2 T. honey
1 to 2 T. Dijon mustard
5 c. shredded coleslaw mix
Optional: 1/4 c. sliced green onions
Optional: 1 jicama, peeled and shredded
1/2 to 1 c. chopped pecans

CREAMY GREEN CHILE ZUCCHINI

MARY COKER
APACHE JUNCTION, AZ

I love anything with a southwestern flair, especially with green chiles! A delicious side dish, or it can be a meatless meal in itself. This is easily doubled and makes a great potluck dish. If you have a mandolin slicer, it works well for slicing the zucchini.

Heat oil in a large skillet over medium heat. Add zucchini and onion; cook until tender, stirring gently. Add chiles and jalapeños; heat through. Add cream cheese; mix through until melted. Sprinkle with shredded cheese; let stand until melted.

Serves 6.

1 T. olive oil
4 zucchini, thinly sliced
1/2 c. onion, diced
4-oz. can diced green chiles
1/4 c. sliced jalapeño peppers
1/2 c. cream cheese, softened
1 c. shredded sharp Cheddar cheese

RAINBOW PASTA SALAD

SUE HAYNES
SCOTTSDALE, AZ

This favorite recipe has been in our family for many years! It's delicious...a great recipe for festive occasions. Make it ahead and just pull it from the fridge at serving time.

16-oz. pkg. tri-colored rotini pasta, uncooked

3 6-oz. jars marinated artichoke hearts, drained

2 12-oz. cans black olives, drained

15-oz. can garbanzo beans, drained

3 to 4 tomatoes, cut into chunks

1/4 lb. sliced Genoa salami, cut into quarters

3 cloves garlic, finely chopped

1/3 c. red wine vinegar

1/3 c. olive oil

1/4 c. canola oil

2 T. dried oregano

3/4 c. grated Parmesan cheese

Cook pasta according to package directions; drain. Transfer to a large bowl while still warm. Add all vegetables, salami and garlic; mix gently. Add remaining ingredients except Parmesan cheese; mix well. Add Parmesan and toss lightly. Cover and refrigerate at least 6 hours before serving.

Serves 8 to 10.

SKILLET SCALLOPED POTATOES

CHARLOTTE FORTIER
LAKESIDE, AZ

I love scalloped potatoes, but sometimes they're just too time-consuming to make. I also wanted to cut back on the calories and fat. So, I made some changes to enjoy the taste of cheesy potatoes in a lighter dish. Sometimes I add diced ham for a quick meal.

Spray a non-stick skillet with non-stick vegetable spray. Add sliced potatoes, onion and pepper, if using. Pour milk or water over top; season with salt and pepper. Turn heat to medium-high. When steam begins to form, reduce heat to low. Cover skillet and cook for 15 to 20 minutes, until potatoes are fork-tender, adding more liquid if needed. Spread cheese over top. Cover and cook over low heat for a few more minutes, until until cheese is melted.

4 potatoes, peeled and thinly sliced

1 onion, thinly sliced

Optional: 1 green pepper, sliced or diced

1/4 c. low-fat milk or water

salt and pepper to taste

1 c. favorite shredded cheese

Serves 4.

FROZEN CRANBERRY SALAD

JOANNE TREYNOR
CHANDLER, AZ

This recipe has been in our family over 60 years and we make it every Thanksgiving and Christmas. We all love it!

Grind cranberries in a food grinder or food processor; do not drain. Combine cranberries and sugar in a bowl; let stand for 2 hours. Stir in marshmallows and pineapple with juice; set aside. In a separate bowl, with an electric mixer on high speed, whip cream until soft peaks form. Add to cranberry mixture; stir well. Transfer to a serving bowl. Cover tightly with plastic wrap, then aluminum foil. Freeze for 3 days. Before serving, thaw in refrigerator all day.

12-oz. pkg. fresh cranberries

1/2 c. sugar

10-oz. pkg. mini marshmallows

15-1/4 oz. can crushed pineapple

1 pt. whipping cream

Serves 14 to 16.

COOL RANCH FIESTA LAYERED TACO SALAD

SHERRY SHEEHAN
PHOENIX, AZ

My ten-layer salad has long been a signature dish. I wanted to make a Tex Mex-style layered salad for variety during long summers when it is often too hot to cook. Plus, I am always on the lookout for meatless dishes to bring to church potlucks for members who are vegetarian. This is my favorite version so far. I use reduced-fat and/or low-sodium ingredients.

- 16-oz. container sour cream
- 1.1-oz. pkg. fiesta ranch dip mix
- 4 c. lettuce, torn
- 1 pt. grape tomatoes
- 2 c. cucumber, peeled and diced
- 15-oz. can black beans, drained and rinsed
- 2 c. red onion, diced
- 15-1/4 oz. can corn, drained
- 2 c. red pepper, diced
- 2 c. shredded Colby Jack cheese, diced
- 2 c. cool ranch tortilla chips, coarsely crushed

Combine sour cream and dip mix in a small bowl. Keep chilled until ready to serve. In a clear glass trifle bowl or serving dish, layer remaining ingredients except tortilla chips in order given, ending with cheese. Spoon sour cream mixture over salad; cover and chill until serving time. Top with tortilla chips just before serving, so they'll stay crisp.

Makes 8 servings.

GRANDMA'S PEAR SALAD

**DANA DOWELL
GLENDALE, AZ**

When I was growing up, my grandmother would make this salad for family get-togethers. I wouldn't try it because I don't like pears very much. When I had my first baby, my family brought me dinner shortly after I was released from the hospital, and my grandma brought along her pear salad. Not wanting to hurt her feelings, I tried a spoonful...I realized that I had missed out on many years of enjoyment by not trying Grandma's Pear Salad earlier!

Place cream cheese, whipped topping and pears in a blender; set aside. Pour boiling water into a small bowl; stir in gelatin until dissolved. Pour gelatin into blender with other ingredients. Blend until well mixed. Pour into an 8-cup serving bowl; refrigerate until set.

Serves 6.

8-oz. pkg. cream cheese, softened

1 c. frozen whipped topping, thawed

15-1/4 oz. can pear halves, drained

1 c. boiling water

3-oz. pkg. lemon gelatin mix

KITCHEN TIP

A dollop of whipped cinnamon butter adds flavor to plain rolls, waffles and breads. Simply blend 2 tablespoons whipped butter with cinnamon.

CRISPY GOLDEN PARMESAN POTATOES

KAREN DAVIS
GLENDALE, AZ

We love potatoes! I'm always tickled to find a tasty new way to fix them. This recipe is scrumptious.

1/4 c. butter, melted and divided
1-3/4 lbs. Yukon gold potatoes, halved lengthwise
1/2 c. grated Parmesan cheese
1 t. garlic powder

Spread one tablespoon melted butter in a 13"x9" baking pan; place remaining butter in a small bowl. Mix cheese and garlic powder in a separate small bowl. Dip cut sides of potatoes into butter, then into cheese mixture. Place cut-side down in baking pan. Drizzle with any remaining butter. Bake, uncovered, at 400 degrees for 30 to 35 minutes, until tender.

Makes 6 to 8 servings.

CUCUMBER CRUNCH SALAD

SHERRY SHEEHAN
PHOENIX, AZ

This salad is very close to my grandmother's recipe. I got an idea from my friend Jill to add additional vegetables to create a lovely red and green salad that's just right with a Christmas ham.

2 cucumbers, peeled and thinly sliced
1 c. red pepper, diced
1 c. green pepper, diced
1 onion, sliced
1/2 c. celery, sliced
1/3 c. cider vinegar
1/3 c. water
3 T. sugar
1/2 t. salt

Combine cucumbers, peppers, onion and celery in a large bowl. In a separate small bowl, combine remaining ingredients; blend well. Pour over vegetable mixture; toss to mix. Chill for at least 2 to 3 hours before serving.

Serves 8.

CHOPPED SALAD

JOELLEN FERINGTON
FOUNTAIN HILLS, AZ

Serve alongside grilled sirloin or hamburgers and fresh-picked ears of sweet corn...scrumptious!

Place tomatoes in a salad serving bowl; toss with mayonnaise and seasonings. Cover and chill for 30 minutes to several hours. At serving time, add lettuce and bacon to bowl. Stir to coat evenly.

Serves 4.

2 tomatoes, coarsely
 chopped
1/3 c. mayonnaise
1/2 t. salt
pepper to taste
1/4 t. cayenne pepper
1 head iceberg lettuce,
 chopped
6 thick slices bacon,
 crisply cooked and
 crumbled

HERBED DEVILED EGGS

MARY GARCIA
PHOENIX, AZ

Deviled eggs are a tasty dish to take to parties. These take the classic taste of deviled eggs and spruce it up a bit with some flavorful fresh herbs and a little spice!

Transfer egg yolks to a bowl and mash; set egg whites aside. Add remaining ingredients to egg yolks; mix well. Fill each egg white half with a tablespoon of filling. Chill at least one hour before serving.

Makes one dozen.

1 doz. eggs, hard-boiled,
 peeled and halved
2 T. fresh chives, minced
2 T. fresh parsley,
 minced
1/4 c. sour cream
1 T. lemon juice
1/2 t. curry powder
salt, pepper and cayenne
 pepper to taste

MOM'S MACARONI & CHEESE

JENNY NEWMAN
GOODYEAR, AZ

My mom has been making this dish since before I was born. As far as I'm concerned, it's the only way to make mac & cheese! I always think of it as a great comfort food, and now I make it for my own family.

8-oz. pkg. elbow
  macaroni, uncooked
5-oz. can evaporated
  milk
1/3 c. water
1 c. milk
3 T. butter
3 T. all-purpose flour
1/2 t. salt
1 T. minced, dried onion
1-1/2 c. shredded sharp
  Cheddar cheese,
  divided

Cook one cup macaroni according to package instructions; drain. Reserve remaining macaroni for another recipe. Combine evaporated milk, water and milk; set aside. Melt butter in a medium saucepan. Add flour and salt, whisking until flour dissolves. Add onion and evaporated milk mixture, stirring well to avoid lumps. Add cheese. Simmer until cheese melts and sauce is thickened, stirring frequently. Stir in cooked macaroni. Pour into a greased 8"x8" baking pan. Top with remaining cheese and bake, uncovered, at 350 degrees for 30 minutes, or until bubbly and lightly golden.

Serves 4 to 6.

CHRISTMAS MARKET POTATOES

PENNY BRYANT
SURPRISE, AZ

When we were stationed in Germany with the Air Force, my husband Ken, our daughter Victoria and I went to the many Christmas markets that every town held during November and December. At every one, this dish was being made right on the street...it was always warm and comforting. Now that we are back in the States, I enjoy making it often.

Heat oil over medium heat in a very large skillet with a lid. Add bacon and cook until almost crisp. Add onions; continue cooking until bacon is done and onions are soft and almost translucent. Add garlic; cook for one to 2 minutes. Add potatoes; cook for 2 to 3 minutes. Using a broad spatula or pancake turner, flatten mixture in skillet. Cook without stirring for 3 minutes; add salt and pepper to taste. Begin turning the mixture over in large sections. Cook on other side until golden. Sprinkle with salt and pepper again as needed.

Makes 6 to 8 servings.

2 T. olive oil

16-oz. pkg. thick-cut bacon, sliced into 1/2-inch pieces

1 to 2 yellow onions, chopped

1 to 2 cloves garlic, chopped

5 lbs. russet potatoes, cubed and cooked

salt and pepper to taste

ZUCCHINI PATTIES

AMBER BRANDT
TUCSON, AZ

Serve with a dollop of sour cream and plenty of salt & pepper.

2 onions, chopped
1 zucchini, grated
6 eggs, beaten
2 c. bread crumbs
**3 T. fresh parsley,
  chopped**
oil for deep frying

Sauté onions in a skillet until tender; add zucchini and cook for 5 minutes, stirring frequently. Remove from heat and set aside. Pour eggs into a large mixing bowl; mix in onion mixture. Stir in bread crumbs and parsley; set aside. Pour 1/4-inch depth oil into a 12" skillet; heat until hot. Drop spoonfuls of zucchini mixture into hot oil until golden on both sides; drain.

Makes 6 to 8 servings.

CHILI RICE

SALLY DAVISON
PAGE, AZ

People love this five-ingredient casserole! It goes well with other southwestern dishes.

3 c. cooked rice
**10-3/4 oz. can cream of
  celery soup**
**4-oz. can diced green
  chiles, or to taste**
**1 c. shredded Monterey
  Jack cheese**
1 c. sour cream
Optional: dried chives

Combine all ingredients except chives. Transfer to a lightly greased 2-quart casserole dish. Bake, uncovered, at 350 degrees for 20 minutes. Garnish with chives, if desired.

Serves 6 to 8.

GRANDMA'S VINTAGE SALAD

MARLA KINNERSLEY
SURPRISE, AZ

This is one of the first recipes Grandma and I would make together in the kitchen. It is really good and has stood the test of time for all of us. We like it as a side salad.

Combine all ingredients in a large bowl, folding in salad dressing last. Serve immediately.

Makes 4 to 6 servings.

1 head iceberg lettuce, chopped

1 c. seedless red grapes, quartered

1 apple, cored and chopped

2 stalks celery, chopped

1/2 c. chopped walnuts

1/4 c. red onion, chopped

6 T. mayonnaise-style salad dressing

CRISPY FRENCH FRIED PARSNIPS

BEV FISHER
MESA, AZ

My mom knew how important it was to get us to eat veggies and looked for new ways to serve them. We found we liked this way!

Toss parsnip strips in oil. Place on ungreased baking sheets and sprinkle with seasonings. Bake at 350 degrees for 30 minutes, turning halfway through, until tender.

Makes 6 to 8 servings.

2 lbs. parsnips, peeled and cut into strips

1/2 t. sea salt or garlic salt

chili powder to taste

3 T. olive oil

HERBED NEW POTATO SALAD

KAREN DAVIS
GLENDALE, AZ

The combination of sage, shallots and thyme really dresses up a crowd favorite.

5 lbs. new potatoes
1 bunch fresh sage
1/2 c. olive oil, divided
salt and pepper to taste
1/4 c. red wine vinegar
3 T. shallots, finely chopped
1 t. fresh thyme, minced
Garnish: fresh sage leaves, sprigs fresh thyme

Place potatoes and sage on a 15"x10" jelly-roll pan; drizzle with 1/4 cup oil and toss gently. Bake at 450 degrees for 35 to 40 minutes, until golden and tender; cool. Halve potatoes and place in a serving bowl; sprinkle with salt and pepper. Crumble roasted sage leaves over potatoes. Whisk together remaining oil, vinegar, shallots and thyme; drizzle over potatoes. Toss to coat. Garnish with fresh sage and thyme sprigs. Chill.

Serves 15.

FARM-STYLE GREEN BEANS

MARY GARCIA
PHOENIX, AZ

Good old-fashioned simmered green beans are delicious! Long cooking over low heat is the secret to the farm-style taste. The beans simmer on the stove while you're doing other things...it's not a recipe to rush! In the summertime, follow these directions using about four pounds of fresh green beans.

4 slices center-cut bacon
1/4 c. butter, sliced
4 14-1/2 oz. cans whole green beans, partially drained
1/8 t. salt

In a large saucepan over medium heat, cook bacon until crisp. Reserve bacon and drippings in skillet. Add green beans along with enough of their liquid to cover the beans. Add butter and salt. Reduce heat to low. Cover and simmer over low heat for 2 to 3 hours. Stir occasionally, checking to make sure beans are still covered with liquid.

Makes 8 to 10 servings.

CHEDDAR POTATO GRATIN

JO ANN
GOOSEBERRY PATCH

Everyone's favorite cheesy potatoes...especially scrumptious with baked ham.

Mix sage, salt and pepper in a cup; set aside. Layer 1/3 of potatoes and half of onion in a lightly greased 13"x9" baking pan. Sprinkle with one teaspoon of sage mixture and 1/3 of cheese. Repeat layers with remaining ingredients, ending with cheese. Whisk cream and broth together until well blended; pour evenly over top. Bake, covered, at 400 degrees for one hour, or until tender and golden. Let stand 5 minutes before serving.

Makes 10 to 12 servings.

2 t. dried sage
1-1/2 t. salt
1/2 t. pepper
3 lbs. potatoes, peeled, thinly sliced and divided
1 onion, thinly sliced and divided
8-oz. pkg. shredded Cheddar cheese, divided
1 c. whipping cream
1 c. chicken broth

DINNERTIME CONVERSATION

With over 2,000 different species of plants, 300 species of birds and 100 species of reptiles and amphibians, Organ Pipe Cactus National Monument is also a biosphere reserve and the only place in the United States where the senita and organ pipe cactus grow wild.

MOM'S BUTTERNUT SQUASH BAKE

SUE ELLEN CRABB
GLENDALE, AZ

My mom got this recipe in a cooking class she took. I remember how delicious it was with fresh veggies from our garden! She made it every Thanksgiving until she passed away, then it became my turn.

10-3/4 oz. can cream of chicken soup
1 c. sour cream
1 c. carrots, peeled and shredded
2 lbs. butternut squash, cooked and lightly mashed
1/4 c. onion, chopped
8-oz. pkg. herb-flavored stuffing mix
1/2 c. butter, melted

In a bowl, combine soup and sour cream; stir in carrots. Fold in squash and onion. Combine stuffing mix and butter; spread 1/2 of mixture in bottom of a lightly greased 3-quart casserole dish. Spoon in squash mixture. Top with remaining stuffing mix. Bake, uncovered, at 350 degrees for 25 to 30 minutes.

Serves 6 to 8.

GERMAN POTATO PANCAKES

ELAINE NICHOLS
MESA, AZ

Garnish with sour cream or applesauce...scrumptious!

4 potatoes, peeled and coarsely grated
1/4 c. milk
1 egg, beaten
1 onion, diced
2 T. all-purpose flour
salt and pepper to taste
oil for frying

Combine all ingredients except oil; mix well with a fork and set aside. Heat 1/4 inch oil in a deep skillet over medium-high heat. For each pancake, spread about 2 heaping tablespoonfuls into a circle in skillet. Cook for 3 to 4 minutes, until golden; turn and cook on other side. Drain on paper towels.

Serves 4 to 6.

SAVORY BRAISED KALE

KAREN DAVIS
GLENDALE, AZ

*Easy and flavorful way to prepare green leafy vegetables...
try it with Swiss chard too!*

In a large skillet over medium heat, cook bacon
until crisp, about 5 minutes. Remove bacon to a
paper towel-lined plate, reserving drippings in skillet.
Crumble bacon and set aside. Increase heat to
medium-high. Add onion to skillet; cook until tender,
about 5 minutes. Add kale; cook until wilted, about
5 minutes, stirring often. Sprinkle cider and vinegar
over kale. Reduce heat to low; cover and cook for
10 minutes, stirring occasionally. Add apple; cook
until apple is tender. Season with salt and pepper. At
serving time, sprinkle with crumbled bacon.

Serves 6.

2 to 3 slices bacon
1-1/4 c. onion, thinly
  sliced
1 lb. fresh kale, chopped
1/3 c. apple cider or
  apple juice
1 T. cider vinegar
1-1/2 c. tart apple, peeled,
  cored and diced
1/2 t. salt
1/4 t. pepper

NIPPY CARROTS

FAYE MAYBERRY
SAINT DAVID, AZ

*I can't resist sharing a recipe from my grandmother. I wasn't too
sure about this dish when I saw the horseradish, but I made it
and it really is flavorful. The sugar balances out the tanginess of
the horseradish and I love it!*

In a medium saucepan, cook carrots in a small
amount of salted water until tender; drain. Add
remaining ingredients and stir gently over low heat
for about 5 minutes, until glazed.

Serves 4.

3 c. carrots, peeled and
  sliced
1 t. prepared
  horseradish
1 T. sugar
2 T. butter salt to taste
1/8 t. pepper

CHAPTER THREE

GRAND CANYON STATE
Soups, Sandwiches & Breads

COZY UP WITH A BOWL OF HEARTY
SOUP AND WARM BREAD OR A TASTY
SANDWICH...PERFECT FOR A COOL
CANYON NIGHT OR ON THE FRONT PORCH
IN YOUR FAVORITE ROCKING CHAIR.

MEXICAN ALBONDIGAS SOUP

SHERRY SHEEHAN
PHOENIX, AZ

My Hispanic pastor tells me this tasty slow-cooker soup tastes just like the soup his mother used to make.

2 lbs. lean ground beef
1 c. Italian-seasoned dry
   bread crumbs
1 egg, beaten
Optional: 1/4 c. olive oil
3 stalks celery, sliced
1 green pepper, diced
1 c. carrots, peeled and
   diced
15-1/4 oz. can corn,
   drained
2 14-oz. cans beef broth
10-oz. can diced
   tomatoes with chiles
4-oz. can diced green
   chiles
3 c. cooked rice
2 T. fresh cilantro,
   finely chopped
2 T. onion, minced
1 t. garlic powder
1 t. ground cumin
1 t. chili powder
1 t. salt
1/2 t. pepper
4 to 5 c. water

Combine ground beef, bread crumbs and egg; form into one-inch balls. Brown in a skillet over medium heat, adding oil if desired; drain. Place meatballs in a slow cooker and set aside. In a small saucepan, cover celery, green pepper and carrots with a little water. Cook until tender; add to slow cooker with remaining ingredients. Cover and cook on low setting for 3 to 4 hours.

Serves 8.

TEX-MEX SLOPPY JOES

ANTHONY FONTANA
SCOTTSDALE, AZ

Wake up your taste buds with this spicy version of an old favorite.

In a skillet over medium heat, brown ground beef, onion and garlic; drain. Combine juice, catsup, water, brown sugar, peppers, mustard and chili powder in a slow cooker; stir in meat mixture. Cover and cook on low setting for 8 to 10 hours. Spoon meat mixture onto buns; garnish as desired.

Makes 8 servings.

1-1/2 lbs. ground beef

1 c. onion, chopped

1 clove garlic, minced

3/4 c. spicy cocktail vegetable juice

3/4 c. catsup

1/2 c. water

2 T. brown sugar, packed

2 T. jalapeño peppers, chopped

1 T. mustard

2 t. chili powder

8 kaiser rolls, split and toasted

Garnish: Mexican-blend shredded cheese, sliced avocado, sliced jalapeño peppers, sliced black olives

VERY VEGGIE CHILI

BOBBIE SOFIA
LAKE HAVASU CITY, AZ

A great healthy recipe to have in the fridge when family comes to visit. Everyone loves it, and it's easy to get a bowlful anytime someone feels hungry!

1 T. olive oil

2 c. carrots, peeled and diced

1 c. celery, diced

1 onion, diced

16-oz. pkg. sliced mushrooms

2 zucchini, chopped

2 yellow squash, chopped

1 T. chili powder

1 t. dried basil

1 t. pepper

4 8-oz. cans tomato sauce

1 c. vegetable broth

2 14-1/2 oz. cans diced tomatoes

2 15-oz. cans black beans, drained and rinsed

2 15-oz. cans dark red kidney beans, drained and rinsed

Optional: 1 c. frozen corn, 2 c. kale or spinach

Heat oil in a large skillet over medium heat. Sauté carrots, celery and onion in oil for 5 minutes. Stir in mushrooms, zucchini and squash; sauté for 3 minutes. Sprinkle with seasonings; cook for 5 minutes. Add tomato sauce and broth to a slow cooker. Add tomatoes with juice, beans, carrot mixture and corn, if using. Cover and cook on low setting for 8 hours. Add kale or spinach during the last hour of cooking, if using.

Serves 6 to 8.

BLUE CHEESE CUT-OUT CRACKERS

ANGELA MURPHY
TEMPE, AZ

Dress up any salad when you serve these rich blue cheese crackers. Make them in any shape you like or cut them into little squares and skip the cookie cutters!

Mix all ingredients together; let rest for 30 minutes. Roll dough out to about 1/8-inch thick. Use small cookie cutters to cut out crackers. 2 Bake on ungreased baking sheets at 400 degrees for 8 to 10 minutes, just until golden. Let cool; remove carefully. Store in an airtight container.

Makes about 2 dozen.

1 c. all-purpose flour
7 T. butter, softened
7 T. crumbled blue cheese
1/2 t. dried parsley
1 egg yolk
4 t. whipping cream
salt and cayenne pepper to taste

GRILLED HAVARTI SANDWICHES

BEV FISHER
MESA, AZ

Now that my children are grown, I'm always looking for recipes that call for ingredients they wouldn't eat. This sandwich is so tasty, I wanted another one the next day after I first tried it!

Spread 4 slices bread on one side with half the butter and all the preserves. Top with cheese, avocado and another slice of bread; spread remaining butter on outside of sandwiches. Heat a large skillet over medium heat. Cook sandwiches for 2 to 3 minutes, until bread is golden and cheese begins to melt. Turn over; press down slightly with a spatula. Cook until golden.

Makes 4 sandwiches.

8 slices French bread
2 t. butter, softened and divided
1/4 c. apricot preserves
1/4 lb. Havarti cheese, sliced
1 avocado, halved, pitted and sliced

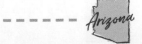

CALIFORNIA AVOCADO SOUP

CHARLOTTE ORM
FLORENCE, AZ

This soup is so pretty and makes a lovely luncheon soup any time of the year.

1/2 c. onion, chopped

1 T. butter

2 14-1/2 oz. cans chicken broth

2 potatoes, peeled and cubed

1/2 t. salt

1/4 t. pepper

2 ripe avocados, halved and pitted

Garnish: sour cream, real bacon bits

In a large saucepan over medium heat, sauté onion in butter until tender. Add broth, potatoes, salt and pepper; bring to a boil. Reduce heat to low. Cover and simmer for 15 to 25 minutes, until potatoes are tender. Remove from heat; cool slightly. Working in batches, scoop avocado pulp into a blender; add potato mixture with broth. Cover and process until puréed. Return to pan; heat through. Garnish with sour cream and bacon bits.

Serves 6.

DINNERTIME CONVERSATION

The original London Bridge was shipped stone-by-stone and reconstructed in Lake Havasu City.

KATHLEEN'S FABULOUS CHILI

KATHY MURRAY STRUNK
MESA, AZ

This recipe is my own creation. It won first place for 'Overall Best Chili' at a church chili cook-off!

Brown ground beef and bacon with onion and green pepper in a skillet over medium heat; drain. Combine all ingredients except garnish in a slow cooker, using half of reserved tomato juice; cover and cook on high setting until chili just begins to simmer, about one hour. Reduce heat to low setting; continue to simmer, covered, for 2 to 4 hours. Add remaining tomato juice if more liquid is needed. Garnish as desired.

Serves 6 to 8.

1 lb. ground beef

1/2 to 1 lb. bacon, chopped

1 onion, chopped

1/2 green pepper, diced

2 15-1/2 oz. cans dark red kidney beans, drained and rinsed

15-1/2 oz. can light red kidney beans, drained and rinsed

15-1/2 oz. can pinto beans

16-oz. can pork & beans

15-1/2 oz. can Sloppy Joe sauce

14-1/2 oz. can diced tomatoes, drained and juice reserved

1/4 to 1/2 c. brown sugar, packed

salt, pepper and chili powder to taste

Garnish: sour cream, sliced green onions, shredded Cheddar cheese

CURLY KALE SOUP

BEV FISHER
MESA, AZ

I love coming up with new soup recipes! It is fun to share with my neighbors. I love to see them enjoy the foods I take to them. If you have homemade broth to use in this recipe, so much the better.

8 c. chicken broth

1-1/2 lbs. fresh kale, ribs discarded and leaves finely chopped

1/2 c. onion, minced

4 eggs, beaten

1/4 c. lemon juice

Garnish: shredded Parmesan cheese

Bring broth to a boil in a heavy saucepan over medium heat. Add kale and onion. Reduce heat to medium-low and simmer until kale is tender, about 20 minutes. Remove pan from heat; allow mixture to cool to room temperature. Once cooled, whisk together eggs and lemon juice in a bowl; whisk into soup. Warm soup over very low heat; do not boil. Ladle soup into bowls. Serve with Parmesan cheese on the side.

Makes 4 servings.

PRESENTATION

For more casual get-togethers, skip the tablecloths and go for brown craft paper instead. Set out markers for guests to keep score, play games and doodle!

SLOW-COOKER CHICKEN CHILI

AMY DELORME
PHOENIX, AZ

My family loves this recipe, and I love it because it is so easy to prepare. It fills up the house with a scrumptious aroma that will get your mouth watering in anticipation.

Combine undrained beans, undrained vegetables, seasoning mix and chicken in a slow cooker. Cover and cook on low setting for 8 hours. Remove chicken from slow cooker; dice or shred. Stir chicken back into soup. Garnish servings with crackers, cheese and diced onion.

Serves 6 to 8.

2 15-1/2 oz. cans black beans

2 15-oz. cans ranch-style beans

28-oz. can stewed tomatoes

15-1/4 oz. can corn

1-1/4 oz. pkg. chili seasoning mix

3 boneless, skinless chicken breasts

Garnish: saltine crackers, shredded Cheddar cheese, diced red onion

TOM'S CHILI CON CARNE

CATHERINE REYNOLDS
SCOTTSDALE, AZ

My dad used to make this chili for us every winter. It's the only time he ever cooked. Daddy called the green pepper a "mango" for reasons he never made clear, even though we told him a mango was something entirely different! Little did we know that that's what some folks used to call green peppers back in Dayton, Ohio, where Dad grew up. This chili is terrific with cornmeal muffins!

1 lb. ground beef
1 onion, diced
1 green pepper, diced
15-oz. can plain or
  seasoned diced
  tomatoes
15-oz. can dark red
  kidney beans
1/2 c. water
2 T. vinegar
1 T. sugar
salt and pepper to taste

Brown beef and onion together in a large skillet over medium heat; drain. Add green pepper, undrained tomatoes and beans, water, vinegar and sugar, stirring after each addition. Reduce heat and simmer for about 30 minutes, stirring occasionally. Individual servings may be seasoned to taste with salt and pepper.

Makes 5 to 6 servings.

KITCHEN TIP

Adding a little pasta water to your sauce before serving will help the sauce cling to the noodles.

BLACK-EYED PEA SOUP

DAYNA JACKSON
MARICOPA, AZ

Whenever I make this soup, I think of my grandma. Grandma always used to give each of us two cans of black-eyed peas at Christmas, to serve on New Year's Day for a new year of prosperity. Some relatives would give me their cans because they didn't care for them. I tried many recipes and finally came up with my own. Sometimes I make chili-cheese cornbread to go with it.

In a skillet over medium heat, cook bacon until lightly crisp. Remove bacon from pan; crumble and set aside. Sauté onion in bacon drippings until tender; drain. In a large saucepan, stir together crumbled bacon, onion, peas with juice, tomatoes with juice, beef broth, salt and pepper. Cook over medium-high heat until nearly boiling; reduce heat to low. Simmer for 20 minutes. Stir in cheese. Continue to simmer over low heat for another 20 minutes. To serve, put a handful of chips in each bowl, ladle soup over chips and sprinkle with cheese.

Serves 4.

5 slices bacon
1/2 c. onion, finely diced
2 15-oz. cans black-eyed peas
10-oz. can diced tomatoes & green chiles
14-oz. can beef broth
salt and pepper to taste
1/2 c. shredded sharp Cheddar cheese
Garnish: tortilla or corn chips, additional shredded Cheddar cheese

SLOW-COOKER SANTA FE SOUP

FAYE MAYBERRY
SAINT DAVID, AZ

I discovered this recipe in a church cookbook, then tweaked it a bit to enhance the flavor and make it my own. This is a quick & easy soup that's just a little step up from the "taco soup" kind of recipes. It feeds a crowd and everyone loves it! If you only have a small crowd, it freezes well.

2 lbs. ground beef

1 onion, chopped

2 1-oz. pkg's. ranch salad dressing mix

2 1-1/4 oz. pkg's. taco seasoning mix

15-1/2 oz. can black beans

15-1/2 oz. can kidney beans

15-1/2 oz. can pinto beans

14-1/2 oz. can diced tomatoes

10-oz. can diced tomatoes with green chiles

2 15-oz. cans yellow or shoepeg corn

tortilla chips

Garnish: shredded cheese, sour cream, sliced green onions, avocados, black olives

In a large skillet over medium heat, cook beef and onion until beef is browned. Drain; stir in salad dressing and seasoning mixes. Transfer beef mixture to a 6-quart slow cooker along with all undrained beans, tomatoes and corn. Cover and cook on low setting for 8 hours. May also simmer in a large soup pot on the stovetop for 2 hours, stirring occasionally. Serve in bowls over crushed tortilla chips; add desired toppings.

Makes about 4 quarts.

MOM'S TURKEY BURGERS

**JENNA ANDERSON
TUCSON, AZ**

Since I moved away from home, my mother's turkey burgers have become a comfort food for me...the yummy smell and taste take me right back home. Super fast...dinner in less than 15 minutes!

In a skillet over medium heat, brown turkey and onion in oil; drain. Add remaining ingredients except buns. Mix together and cook until heated through. Serve on hamburger buns.

Makes 4 to 6 servings.

1 lb. ground turkey
1 onion, chopped
1 to 2 T. oil
10-3/4 oz. can chicken gumbo soup
2 T. mustard
1 T. catsup
1/2 t. salt
4 to 6 hamburger buns, split

CAROL'S BEEF BOATS

**CAROL JORDAN
GILBERT, AZ**

I developed this sandwich recipe twenty years ago when my kids were young...it has stood the test of time! They are speedy to make, easy to take and can feed a crowd.

Brown beef and onion in a large skillet over medium heat. Drain; add salt and pepper to taste. Add soup and heat through. Stir in cheese; cook until melted. Hollow out bottoms of rolls. Spoon beef mixture into rolls and replace tops. Wrap sandwiches individually in aluminum foil. Bake at 350 degrees for 15 minutes.

Makes 12 sandwiches.

2 lbs. ground beef
1 c. shredded Cheddar cheese
1 onion, finely chopped
12 French rolls, split
salt and pepper to taste
10-3/4 oz. can cream of mushroom soup

BUCK-A-ROO-STEW

FAYE MAYBERRY
BENSON, AZ

I found this easy chili-like recipe in an old church cookbook. I changed it a bit and spiced it up to give it some great flavor. My family loves it! We like to top it with cheese and enjoy it with tortilla chips.

2 lbs. ground beef
1-1/2 c. onions, diced
28-oz. can crushed
  tomatoes
15-1/2 oz. can black
  beans, drained
16-oz. pkg. frozen corn
8-oz. jar medium or hot
  salsa
2 t. ground cumin
1/2 t. garlic powder

In a large skillet over medium heat, brown beef with onions; drain. Stir in remaining ingredients and bring to a simmer. Reduce heat to medium-low. Simmer for 30 minutes, stirring occasionally.

Serves 8 to 10.

EASY BEAN STEW

LINDA SMITH
FOUNTAIN HILLS, AZ

This is a wonderful hearty slow-cooker stew, very tasty yet so simple to make. While living in the midwest, we made it often in the fall and winter...it always seemed to hit the spot! If you use extra-lean beef or turkey like I do, there's no need to brown it first. Mix & match your favorite canned beans as you like.

2 lbs. extra-lean ground
  beef or ground turkey
3 15-oz. cans pinto or
  kidney beans, drained
2 10-3/4 oz. cans tomato
  soup
10-3/4 oz. can Cheddar
  cheese soup
salt and pepper to taste

Crumble uncooked beef or turkey into a 6-quart slow cooker. Add remaining ingredients; stir well. Cover and cook on low setting for 6 to 8 hours, or on high setting for 3 to 4 hours.

Makes 8 to 10 servings.

CRAB SALAD CROISSANTS

**MARLA KINNERSLEY
SURPRISE, AZ**

We're always trying to eat healthier at our house, so I came up with this delicious crab salad. It's great on wheat croissants...too good not to share with friends!

In a bowl, combine all ingredients except croissants and garnish. Top each croissant bottom with a lettuce slice; spread evenly with crab salad and top with avocado slices.

Makes 4 sandwiches.

2 8-oz. pkgs. flake-style imitation crabmeat, chopped

2-1/4 oz. can sliced black olives, drained

1 stalk celery, finely chopped

2 T. red onion, finely chopped

1/4 c. light mayonnaise

juice of 1/2 lemon

1-1/2 t. ranch salad dressing mix

4 wheat croissants, split

Garnish: leafy green lettuce, sliced avocado

KITCHEN TIP

Keep a small strainer handy for easily juicing citrus fruits right into the bowl.

BBQ SLOPPY JOES

FAYE MAYBERRY
SAINT DAVID, AZ

The barbecued beans give this recipe such a unique flavor. We like to eat these sandwiches with corn chips tucked inside for a little crunch in every bite.

1 lb. ground beef
1/2 onion, chopped
28-oz. can barbecued beans
14-1/2 oz. can stewed tomatoes
1-1/2 oz. pkg. Sloppy Joe mix
6 sandwich buns, split and toasted

Brown beef and onion in a skillet over medium heat; drain. Stir in remaining ingredients except buns; simmer for about 30 minutes. Serve over toasted buns.

Serve 6.

GIOVANNI'S CHILI

FAYE MAYBERRY
SAINT DAVID, AZ

This is a satisfying meal our family enjoys whenever we go backpacking or camping. We love to camp and a lot of our favorite memories are of these family trips. This recipe is terrific, and so easy to make.

16-oz. pkg. spaghetti, uncooked
1/2 t. salt
2 T. chili seasoning mix
2 T. taco seasoning mix
7-oz. env. brown gravy mix
3 c. water

Measure out half the package of spaghetti and break in half; reserve the rest for another use. Combine all ingredients except water in a plastic zipping bag; shake to combine. In a soup pot or Dutch oven set on a campfire grate, bring water to a boil. Add dry ingredients from bag and cook until spaghetti is tender, about 8 to 10 minutes. Add more water if necessary to thin to desired consistency.

Makes 4 servings.

BEAN & SAUSAGE SOUP

JANICE MARSHALL
TUCSON, AZ

My dad just loves this soup! Your house will smell wonderful as it's cooking. Serve it with a big buttery piece of cornbread and you have a wonderful cool-weather meal.

In a large saucepan or soup pot over medium heat, cook sausage in olive oil until browned. Cut sausage into bite-size pieces; set aside in a bowl. Add prosciutto or ham, onions, carrots, celery and thyme to skillet; cook until soft. Mash one can of beans with a fork; add to pan along with remaining beans and broth. Return sausage to saucepan. Reduce heat to low; cover and simmer for about one hour, stirring occasionally.

Serves 4 to 6.

1-1/2 lbs. mild or spicy Italian pork sausage links

2 T. olive oil

1/4 lb. prosciutto or deli ham, chopped

2 onions, chopped

3 carrots, peeled and chopped

3 stalks celery, chopped

1 t. ground thyme

3 15-oz. cans Great Northern beans, drained, rinsed and divided

4 c. chicken broth

PARMESAN-GARLIC BISCUITS

JO ANN
GOOSEBERRY PATCH

These upside-down biscuits are a hit with any Italian dish!

Coat bottom of a 9" pie pan with butter; add celery seed and garlic. Slice each biscuit into quarters; arrange on top of butter mixture. Sprinkle with Parmesan cheese; bake at 425 degrees for 12 to 15 minutes. Invert onto a serving plate to serve.

Makes 8 servings.

3 T. butter, melted

12-oz. tube refrigerated biscuits

1/4 t. celery seed

2 T. grated Parmesan cheese

2 cloves garlic, minced

MUFFULETTA SANDWICH

SHERYL BEYER
ORO VALLEY, AZ

The perfect sandwich for game day! Feeds a crowd and it's so easy to tuck into the tailgating cooler.

1/4 c. red wine vinegar
2 cloves garlic, minced
1 t. dried oregano
1/3 c. olive oil
10 large green olives, chopped
1/3 c. Kalamata olives, chopped
1/4 c. roasted red pepper, chopped
salt and pepper to taste
1 round loaf sourdough bread
1/4 lb. sliced deli ham
1/4 lb. sliced deli mortadella
1/4 lb. sliced deli salami
1/4 lb. deli sliced Pepper Jack cheese
1/4 lb. Cheddar cheese, sliced
1 to 2 c. lettuce or spinach leaves

In a large bowl, whisk together vinegar, garlic and oregano; gradually blend in olive oil. Stir in olives, red pepper, salt and pepper. Set aside. Cut off top of loaf and hollow out the center. Spread half of olive mixture inside loaf. Layer with meats and cheeses; top with lettuce or spinach. Add remaining olive mixture; cover with top of loaf. Press down firmly; wrap tightly with plastic wrap. Refrigerate at least one hour. Slice into wedges.

Serves 8.

MEATBALL VEGETABLE SOUP

SALLY DERKENNE
CHANDLER, AZ

The made-from-scratch meatballs are really tasty, but if time is short, substitute frozen meatballs

Combine broth and water in a large soup pot. Add celery, carrots, onion, barley, tomato sauce, basil and bouillon cubes; bring to a boil. Reduce heat; partially cover and simmer for 15 minutes. Add meatballs; cover and cook for 15 minutes. Add potatoes and cook until tender, about 20 minutes. Add salt and pepper to taste.

Serves 6.

Meatballs:
Combine all ingredients in a large bowl; mix well. Shape into small meatballs.

4 c. beef broth
2-1/2 c. water
4 stalks celery, chopped
4 carrots, peeled and chopped
1 onion, chopped
1/4 c. quick-cooking barley, uncooked
8-oz. can tomato sauce
1 t. dried basil
2 cubes beef bouillon
3 potatoes, peeled and cubed
salt and pepper to taste

MEATBALLS
1-1/2 lbs. ground beef
1/2 c. cooked rice
1 onion, finely chopped
1 egg, beaten
1/4 c. water
1 clove garlic, minced
salt and pepper to taste

SWISS STEAK STEW

DEBBIE DEVERILL
GILBERT, AZ

This satisfying slow-cooker stew is easy to prepare. As it cooks, your whole house smells just wonderful too!

1/4 c. all-purpose flour

1/2 t. salt

1-1/2 lbs. beef round steak, cut into bite-size pieces

3 c. new red potatoes, peeled and quartered

1 onion, diced

1 clove garlic, minced

14-1/2 oz. can Italian-style diced tomatoes

3/4 c. beef broth or water

1 c. canned sliced carrots

1 c. canned corn

1 c. canned green beans

Mix flour and salt together in a shallow bowl. Add beef; toss to coat well. Spray a skillet with non-stick vegetable spray; heat over medium heat. Brown beef on all sides. In a slow cooker, layer potatoes, beef, onion and garlic. Stir together tomatoes, broth or water and any remaining flour mixture; pour over top. Cover and cook on low setting for 7 to 8 hours, until beef is tender. Add remaining vegetables and cook until warmed through, about 10 to 15 minutes.

Makes 6 servings.

SPARKLING BERRY SOUP

JO ANN
GOOSEBERRY PATCH

"Berry" refreshing...use your favorite in this recipe.

Purée berries and juices together; pour into a punch bowl. Stir in sugar and sparkling water; cover and refrigerate for 2 hours. Ladle into chilled serving bowls; top with a scoop of ice cream or frozen yogurt, if desired.

Makes 6 to 8 servings.

6 c. berries, stems removed
1 c. orange juice
3 T. lemon juice
1/2 c. sugar
2 c. sparkling water
Optional: ice cream or frozen yogurt

FAMOUS HIDDEN SANDWICH

KAREN DAVIS
GLENDALE, AZ

I have fond memories of lunching at the old department store downtown with my best friend. This sandwich was a favorite. You'll need a knife and fork!

Place bread slice on a plate. Layer with ham, cheese and turkey slices. Mound shredded lettuce on top. Cover with salad dressing. Top with egg slices and tomato slices; criss-cross bacon slices on top. Garnish with sweet pickle slices.

Makes one sandwich.

1 slice rye bread
1 slice deli ham
1 slice Swiss cheese
1 slice deli turkey
1 c. lettuce, shredded
1/2 c. Russian or Thousand Island salad dressing
1 egg, hard-boiled, peeled and sliced
2 slices tomato
2 slices bacon, crisply cooked
Garnish: sweet pickle slices

WHITE BEAN & PESTO SOUP

MARY GARCIA
PHOENIX, AZ

Earthy, satisfying and takes no time at all to make! Serve with a hot loaf of crusty bread.

3 15-1/2 oz. cans
cannellini beans,
drained and rinsed

2-1/2 to 3 c. chicken
broth, divided

1/4 c. shredded
Parmesan cheese,
divided

8 to 10 sun-dried
tomatoes in water,
drained and sliced

1/3 c. pesto sauce

salt and pepper to taste

In a large saucepan, combine beans and 1-1/2 cups broth. Bring to a boil over medium-high heat. Reduce heat to medium-low. Simmer for 8 to 10 minutes, until thickened. Stir in 3 tablespoons cheese and remaining ingredients; add remaining broth to desired consistency. Heat through, but do not boil. Garnish with remaining cheese.

Makes 6 servings.

JUST FOR FUN

Arizona, among all the states, has the largest percentage of its land set aside and designated as American Indian lands.

MOM'S ZUCCHINI BREAD

**JAMIE TOMKINS
LAKESIDE, AZ**

My mom has made this bread for years and when I finally moved out, she gave me the recipe to make for my own family. It's great to bake something yummy that has some health benefits too, especially for a kid who doesn't know there's zucchini inside. Shh!

Beat eggs in a bowl. Add oil, sugar, zucchini and vanilla; blend together. In a separate bowl, mix remaining ingredients except nuts. Add to egg mixture; stir well. Fold in nuts. Divide batter between 2 greased 9"x5" loaf pans, filling 1/2 to 3/4 full. Bake at 325 degrees for one hour, or until a toothpick inserted in the center comes out clean. Turn out loaves onto a wire rack to cool.

Makes 2 loaves.

3 eggs
1 c. oil
2 c. sugar
2 c. zucchini, grated
2 t. vanilla extract
3 c. all-purpose flour
1 t. baking powder
1 t. baking soda
1 t. salt
1 t. cinnamon
1/2 c. chopped nuts

COLD-DAY VEGETABLE STEW

MARY GARCIA
PHOENIX, AZ

We always make this stew when we take fall camping trips!

28-oz. can Italian peeled whole tomatoes, drained and liquid reserved

14-1/2 oz. can vegetable or chicken broth

4 redskin potatoes, cut into 1/2-inch cubes

1-1/2 c. carrots, peeled and cut into 1/2-inch pieces

12 oz. bag of frozen corn

1 c. onion, peeled and diced

16 oz. container of baby Bella mushrooms, washed and sliced

1/2 t. salt

1/2 t. dried thyme

1/2 t. dried rosemary

3 T. cornstarch

3 T. cold water

Coarsely chop tomatoes and add to a 5-quart slow cooker along with reserved liquid. Add remaining ingredients except cornstarch and cold water. Cover and cook on low setting for 8 to 10 hours. About 30 minutes before serving, dissolve cornstarch in cold water; gradually stir into stew until well blended. Cover and cook on high setting about 20 minutes, stirring occasionally, until thickened.

Makes 8 servings.

FIREMAN'S BEEF BARLEY SOUP

SHIRLEY MURRAY
TUCSON, AZ

Hearty and satisfying...real old-fashioned goodness!

Heat oil in a large soup pot over medium-high heat; add beef. Brown beef on all sides; drain and set beef aside in a bowl. Add onion and celery to soup pot. Sauté until tender; cover and cook over medium heat for 5 minutes. Return beef to soup pot along with undrained tomatoes and remaining ingredients. Bring to a boil. Reduce heat to low; cover and simmer for 1-1/2 hours, stirring occasionally. Discard bay leaves before serving.

Serves 6 to 8.

2 T. oil

1 to 2 lbs. beef flank steak, cut into 1/2-inch cubes

1/2 c. onion, diced

3 stalks celery, diced

14-1/2 oz. can diced tomatoes with garlic & onion

5 c. beef broth

1 c. long-cooking pearled barley, uncooked

1/4 c. fresh parsley, chopped

1 T. Worcestershire sauce

3 bay leaves

1 t. fresh thyme, snipped

salt and pepper to taste

CHAPTER FOUR

MONUMENT VALLEY
Mains

FILL THEM UP WITH A YUMMY,

STICK-TO-THE-RIBS MEAL THAT IS

HEARTY ENOUGH TO SATISFY EVEN

THE BIGGEST APPETITE.

MOM'S HOMEMADE PIZZA

ANGELA MURPHY
TEMPE, AZ

Nothing is better than homemade pizza!

8-oz. can tomato sauce
1/2 t. sugar
1/4 t. pepper
1 t. garlic powder
1-1/2 t. dried thyme
3 T. grated Parmesan
cheese
1 onion, finely chopped
5 roma tomatoes, sliced
1 c. fresh spinach,
chopped
1 c. shredded part-skim
mozzarella cheese

PIZZA DOUGH
1 env. quick-rise yeast
1 c. hot water
2 T. olive oil
1/2 t. salt
3 c. all-purpose flour,
divided
1 T. cornmeal

Prepare Pizza Dough. Combine tomato sauce, sugar and seasonings; spread over dough. Top with Parmesan cheese, onion, tomatoes, spinach and shredded cheese. Bake at 400 degrees for 25 to 30 minutes, until edges are golden.

Makes 10 servings.

Pizza Dough:
Combine yeast and water. Let stand 5 minutes. Add olive oil, salt and half of the flour. Stir to combine. Stir in remaining flour. Gather into a ball and place in oiled bowl. Turn dough over and cover with plastic wrap. Let rise 30 minutes. Brush oil over a 15"x10" sheet pan or 2, 12" round pizza pans; sprinkle with cornmeal. Roll out dough; place on pan.

MAKE-AHEAD
CHICKEN-CHILE ROLLS

**MARY GARCIA
PHOENIX, AZ**

Make this scrumptious casserole the night before, refrigerate it overnight and pop it in the oven the next evening...what a timesaver!

Flatten chicken breasts to 1/4-inch thick between pieces of wax paper. Top each piece of chicken with one strip of cheese and 2 tablespoons chiles; roll up. Combine bread crumbs, Parmesan cheese and seasonings in a bowl; place melted butter in a separate bowl. Dip chicken rolls in butter and coat in crumb mixture. Arrange chicken rolls in a lightly greased 13"x9" baking pan, seam-side down; drizzle with any remaining butter. Cover and chill overnight. The next day, uncover and bake at 400 degrees for 30 minutes, until heated through. Shortly before serving time, warm enchilada sauce in a saucepan or in the microwave; ladle sauce evenly over chicken. Garnish as desired.

Serves 6.

6 boneless, skinless chicken breasts
1/4 lb. Monterey Jack cheese, cut into 6 strips
7-oz. jar diced chiles, divided
1/2 c. dry bread crumbs
1/2 c. grated Parmesan cheese
1 T. chili powder
1/2 t. salt
1/4 t. pepper
1/4 t. ground cumin
1/4 c. plus 2 T. butter, melted
2 c. enchilada sauce
Garnish: shredded Mexican-blend cheese, sour cream, diced tomatoes, green onions

HEARTY TORTILLA CASSEROLE

ANGELA MURPHY
TEMPE, AZ

A hint of coffee brings a warm heartiness to this dish!

2 lbs. ground beef
1 onion, chopped
2 t. instant coffee granules
1 t. salt
1 t. pepper
1 T. chili powder
29-oz. can tomato sauce, divided
12 10-inch flour tortillas
1/2 c. cream cheese, softened
1/3 c. water
2 c. shredded Cheddar or mozzarella cheese
12 black olives, sliced

Brown beef and onion in a skillet over medium heat; drain. Add coffee granules, seasonings and half the tomato sauce to beef mixture; set aside. Spread each tortilla with cream cheese. Add 1/4 cup of beef mixture to each tortilla and fold over. Place folded tortillas in a greased 13"x9" baking pan. Top with any remaining beef mixture. In a bowl, combine water and remaining tomato sauce; drizzle over tortillas. Sprinkle cheese and olives on top. Cover with aluminum foil and bake at 375 degrees for about 25 minutes, until heated through.

Serves 6 to 8.

Whether you are looking for a quick breakfast to start the day off right, no-fuss party fare for those special guests, satisfying soups and sandwiches for the perfect lunch, main dishes to bring them to the table fast, or a sweet little something to savor at the end of the meal, you'll love these recipes from the amazing cooks in beautiful Arizona.

1y Mom's Muffin Doughnuts, p14

amous Hidden Sandwich, p71

California Avocado Soup, p56

ery Veggie Chili, p54

Caramel Fudge Brownies, p130

Scalloped Potatoes, p31

Tex-Mex Sloppy Joes, p53

Mom's Homemade Pizza, p78

led Havarti Sandwiches, p55

ed Chicken Enchiladas, p88

Chili Rice, p44

Make-Ahead Chicken-Chile Rolls, p79

Triple-Layered Brownies, p130

Blue-Ribbon Pecan Pie, p136

Super Berry Crisp, p131

Blue Cheese Cut-Out Crackers, p55

Kathleen's Fabulous Chili, p57

Hearty Tortilla Casserole, p80

Blueberry–Lemon Crepes, p23

Fried Cheese Sticks, p117

Dijon-Ginger Carrots, p31

Slow-Cooker Apple Cake, p142

CURRIED CHICKEN-BROCCOLI CASSEROLE

**KATHY ARNER
PHOENIX, AZ**

My wonderful mother-in-law fixed this quick recipe all the time. Also terriffic with turkey leftovers at the holidays. If you make this ahead of time, place the casserole in the oven as it preheats to gradually heat up. Serve with fresh rolls, fruit or salad.

In a bowl, combine soup, lemon juice, curry powder and mayonnaise. Place broccoli in a greased 9"x9" baking pan. Add chicken. Pour soup mixture over chicken; stir to mix all. Top with Cheddar cheese and sprinkle bread crumbs on top. Bake, uncovered, at 350 degrees for 45 minutes, or until golden and bubbly.

Serves 4 to 6.

10-3/4 oz. can cream of chicken soup
1 t. lemon juice
1/4 to 1/2 t. curry powder
1/2 c. mayonnaise
10-oz. pkg. frozen chopped broccoli, thawed and drained
2 c. chicken, cooked and chopped
1 c. shredded Cheddar cheese
1/4 c. dry bread crumbs

JUST FOR FUN

At one time, camels were used to transport goods across Arizona.

BAKED CHICKEN ENCHILADAS

ANGELA MURPHY
TEMPE, AZ

My family is nuts for Mexican food. So I came up with this recipes that I can make ahead and freeze to have ready anytime our cravings for Mexican food sets in.

2 c. cooked chicken, chopped or shredded

1 c. salsa or picante sauce

2 c. shredded Cheddar cheese

4 green onions, chopped

1-1/2 t. ground cumin

1 t. dried oregano

8 8-inch flour tortillas

2 T. butter, melted

Garnish: additional shredded cheese, green onions, salsa

In a bowl, combine chicken, salsa or sauce, cheese, onions and seasonings. Spoon 1/3 cup of mixture down the center of each tortilla; fold opposite sides over filling. Roll up from bottom and place seam-side down on an ungreased baking sheet. Brush with melted butter. Bake, uncovered, at 400 degrees for 30 minutes, or until golden, turning halfway through cooking. Garnish with additional cheese and onions; serve with salsa on the side, as desired.

Serves 4 to 6.

Arizona

TUNA NOODLE CRISP

FAYE MAYBERRY
BENSON, AZ

This is a recipe I found in my grandmother's stash of recipes that I've inherited. It's a cheesy little twist on the old classic, tuna noodle casserole. The pimentos give great color!

Cook noodles according to package directions; drain. Meanwhile, add oil to a large skillet over medium heat. Add onion and green pepper; cook until tender. Stir in soup, milk, salt, pepper and pimentos, if using; bring to a boil. Fold in cooked noodles and tuna. Transfer mixture to a lightly greased 1-1/2 or 2-quart casserole dish. Sprinkle bread crumbs on top. Bake, uncovered, at 350 degrees for 25 to 30 minutes, until hot and bubbly.

Serves 4 to 6.

2 c. wide egg noodles, uncooked

2 t. oil

1/3 c. onion, chopped

2 T. green pepper, chopped

10-3/4 oz. can Cheddar cheese soup

1/2 c. milk

1 t. salt

1/8 t. pepper

Optional: 1 T. chopped pimentos, drained

6-oz. can tuna, drained and flaked

1/2 c. dry bread crumbs

KITCHEN TIP

Buy pre-peeled garlic and keep cloves individually wrapped in the freezer.

VAGABOND CHICKEN BUNDLES

JANICE MARSHALL
TUCSON, AZ

I used to love hobo hamburger packs when I was a Girl Scout and went camping. Then I figured out this version with chicken and squash...it's perfect for summertime meals.

1 T. olive oil
3 c. zucchini, sliced
3 c. yellow squash, sliced
6 boneless, skinless chicken breasts
Italian seasoning and pepper to taste
2 c. shredded mozzarella cheese

Brush six 10-inch lengths of heavy-duty aluminum foil with olive oil. Top each square with 1/2 cup zucchini and and 1/2 cup squash. Cut several slits in each chicken breast with a knife tip; lay on top of squash. Sprinkle with seasonings. Top chicken evenly with cheese. Wrap bundles lightly in foil. Grill over medium-high heat for 30 minutes, or until chicken juices run clear.

Serves 6.

CORNBREAD CHICKEN CASSEROLE

CLARA KING
MARICOPA, AZ

I have given out this recipe numerous times to friends. The pastor's wife loved my recipe so much she printed it in the church bulletin!

14-oz. pkg. herb stuffing crumbs
1/2 c. butter, melted
2 lbs. chicken breasts, cooked and shredded
1/2 c. half-and-half
10-3/4 oz. can cream of chicken soup
10-3/4 oz. can cream of mushroom soup
14-1/2 oz. can chicken broth

In a large bowl, combine stuffing crumbs and butter. Mix well; reserve one cup crumbs. Spread remaining mixture in a lightly greased 13"x9" baking pan. Layer with shredded chicken. In a separate bowl, blend half-and-half and soups; spread over chicken. Sprinkle with reserved crumbs. Pour chicken broth evenly over top. Cover with aluminum foil. Bake at 350 degrees for 30 minutes. Uncover; bake 20 minutes longer.

Serves 8.

EVERYTHING-BUT-THE-KITCHEN-SINK MEXICAN CHICKEN

EMILY SALSKY
MESA, AZ

This is my go-to chicken recipe for all kinds of Mexican meals! Use it to fill enchiladas, quesadillas or chalupas, or serve it over rice with cheese. It's easy, nutritious and best of all, delicious.

Combine all ingredients in a 5-quart slow cooker; stir to mix well. Cover and cook on low setting for 8 hours. Shred chicken with a fork; stir back into mixture in slow cooker. Serve as desired.

Makes 6 servings.

2 to 3 boneless, skinless chicken breasts
1 green pepper, chopped
1 red pepper, chopped
1 onion, chopped
16-oz. jar favorite salsa
10-oz. pkg. frozen corn
10-oz. can diced tomatoes with green chiles
Optional: 15-1/2 oz. can black or pinto beans
1-oz. pkg. taco seasoning mix
ground cumin, salt and pepper to taste

TALLARINE CASSEROLE

SUE ROBERSON
PEORIA, AZ

My mom used to serve this yummy casserole when I was growing up...it has been in my family for over 40 years. Its name comes from a Spanish word for noodles.

8-oz. pkg. wide egg noodles, uncooked and divided

1 lb. lean ground beef

1 onion, diced

2 10-3/4 oz. cans tomato soup

15-1/4 oz. can corn, drained

8-oz. pkg. shredded Cheddar cheese, divided

Measure out 2 cups noodles and cook according to package directions. Reserve remaining noodles for another recipe. Brown beef and onion in a skillet over medium heat; drain. Combine cooked noodles, beef mixture, soup and corn in a greased 2-quart casserole dish; stir in one cup cheese. Mix well and top with remaining cheese. Bake, uncovered, at 350 degrees for 30 minutes, or until bubbly.

Serves 6.

YUMMY HAM & SWEET POTATOES

LINDA SMITH
FOUNTAIN HILLS, AZ

One of my family's favorite slow-cooker recipes for fall! It's very easy to make and tastes wonderful. Currently I'm cooking for just my husband and myself...this recipe is just right for the two of us.

2 to 4 small sweet potatoes

1/4 c. brown sugar, packed

1-1/2 lb. boneless ham

1/2 t. dry mustard

Place unpeeled sweet potatoes in a 4-quart slow cooker. Place ham on top. Blend together brown sugar and mustard; spread over ham. Cover and cook on low setting for 3 to 6 hours, until sweet potatoes are tender and a meat thermometer inserted in thickest part of ham reads 145 degrees. To serve, peel sweet potatoes, if desired. Slice ham and sweet potatoes; serve topped with juices from slow cooker.

Makes 2 to 4 servings.

RANCH CHICKEN & NOODLES

BEV FISHER
MESA, AZ

Most people like chicken and will enjoy this recipe as much as I do. When I serve it to company, they always ask for the recipe.

In a skillet over medium heat, cook bacon until crisp. Drain bacon on paper towels; reserve 2 tablespoons drippings in skillet. Cook chicken in reserved drippings until tender and golden on all sides. Sprinkle flour and dressing mix over chicken in skillet; stir in milk. Cook and stir until thickened and bubbly. Cook and stir for one minute more. Stir in bacon. Serve chicken and sauce over cooked noodles, sprinkled with cheese.

Serves 4.

6 slices bacon, cut into narrow strips

4 boneless, skinless chicken breasts, cut into bite-size pieces

2 T. all-purpose flour

2 T. ranch salad dressing mix

1-1/4 c. milk

8-oz. pkg. medium egg noodles, cooked

Garnish: grated Parmesan cheese

PRESENTATION

Piping homemade whipped cream through a piping bag, instead of a dollop, adds a pretty touch to any dessert or breakfast treat.

DEB'S CHICKEN FLORENTINE

DEB EATON
MESA, AZ

My husband loves Italian food! When a local restaurant closed, he was sad that he couldn't get his favorite dish anymore, so I recreated it for him at home. You can substitute frozen spinach, canned mushrooms or leftover rotisserie chicken. Serve with garlic bread sticks hot from the oven to sop up all the delicious juices!

16-oz. pkg. linguine
  pasta, uncooked
2 T. olive oil
3 cloves garlic, minced
4 boneless, skinless
  chicken breasts, thinly
  sliced
1-1/4 c. fat-free zesty
  Italian salad dressing,
  divided
8 sun-dried tomatoes,
  chopped
8-oz. pkg. sliced
  mushrooms
5-oz. pkg. baby spinach
cracked pepper to taste
Optional: grated
  Parmesan cheese,
chopped fresh flat-leaf
  parsley

Cook pasta according to package directions; drain. While pasta is cooking, warm oil in a skillet over medium heat. Add garlic and cook 2 minutes. Add chicken; cook until no longer pink. Drizzle chicken with one cup salad dressing. Stir in tomatoes and mushrooms; cover skillet and simmer until mushrooms are softened. Add spinach; cover skillet again. Cook another 2 to 3 minutes, just until spinach is wilted; stir and sprinkle with pepper. Toss cooked linguine with remaining salad dressing. Serve chicken and vegetables over linguine, garnished as desired.

Makes 6 servings.

LINGUINE & VEGETABLES

ELAINE NICHOLS
MESA, AZ

This super-quick dish is a great alternative to the usual pasta & tomato sauce...give it a try and I think you'll agree!

Heat oil in a large skillet over medium heat. Add uncooked linguine; cook and stir until golden. Add onion, garlic and seasonings; simmer for about 5 minutes. Stir in one can broth and simmer until linguine is tender, adding the other can as needed. Add all vegetables; simmer until vegetables are tender. Drain; sprinkle with cheese before serving.

Serves 6.

1 T. olive oil

16-oz. pkg. linguine pasta, uncooked and broken up

1/2 c. onion, finely chopped

2 cloves garlic, minced

1 T. Italian seasoning

salt and pepper to taste

2 14-oz. cans vegetable broth, divided

14-1/2 oz. can Italian-seasoned diced tomatoes, drained

16-oz. pkg. frozen Italian-blend vegetables

4-oz. can button mushrooms, drained

Garnish: grated Parmesan cheese

MOLLY'S TEX-MEX DINNER

ANGELA MURPHY
TEMPE, AZ

*My roommate tossed this together before leaving for an early-morning
class. By lunchtime, it was ready, and tasted great!*

3/4 c. cornmeal

1-1/2 c. milk

1 egg, beaten

1 lb. ground beef,
  browned and drained

1-1/4 oz. pkg. chili
  seasoning mix

1 t. seasoned salt

14-1/2 oz. can diced
  tomatoes

15-1/4 oz. can corn,
  drained

2-1/4 oz. can sliced black
  olives, drained

8-oz. pkg. shredded
  Mexican-blend cheese

Mix together cornmeal, milk and egg in a large bowl.
Stir in remaining ingredients except cheese; spoon
into a slow cooker. Cover and cook on high setting
for 3 to 4 hours. Sprinkle with cheese; cover and
continue to cook for an additional 5 to 10 minutes,
until cheese melts.

Serves 6.

HOT WING-SPICY CHICKEN

KATHY SKOGEN
PEORIA, AZ

*We love hot chicken wings. This is an easy way to enjoy the same
spicy flavor without the mess of the wings!*

4 to 6 boneless, skinless
  chicken breasts

1 c. butter, melted

1 c. cayenne hot pepper
  sauce

Arrange chicken in a slow cooker. Mix melted butter
and hot sauce; drizzle over chicken. Cover and cook
on low setting for 5 to 6 hours. Chicken may also be
baked, covered, at 350 degrees for about one hour.

Serves 4 to 6.

LEMON GARLIC CHICKEN

KIMBERLY MARLATT
YUMA, AZ

*This dish is so versatile, super-easy to make and pleasing to even
the pickiest of palates. For a side, you can cook up some stir-fry
veggies with a bit of the sauce and serve everything over hot rice...
yummy!*

Spray a 6-quart slow cooker with non-stick vegetable spray; add chicken. In a bowl, combine remaining ingredients except cornstarch and water. Pour over chicken; stir. Cover and cook on high setting for one hour. Reduce heat to low; cook for 3 to 4 hours. To thicken sauce, combine cornstarch and water; stir into slow cooker. Cover and cook for 10 minutes longer, or until sauce thickens.

Serves 6 to 8.

6 to 8 boneless, skinless chicken thighs
2/3 c. soy sauce
1/3 c. lemon or lime juice
2 T. Worcestershire sauce
2 t. rice wine vinegar
1-1/2 t. garlic powder
1 t. sugar
1/2 t. pepper
1/2 t. dry mustard
Optional: 1 to 2 T. cornstarch, 1 to 2 T. cold water

 ALL-TIME-FAVORITE RECIPES FROM ARIZONA COOKS **97**

SKILLET TURKEY CHILAQUILES

ANGELA MURPHY
TEMPE, AZ

It's good to know something different to do with leftover turkey! You may even have broken-up tortilla chips left after watching the big game on TV. Enjoy!

2 T. olive oil

1-1/2 c. red onion, diced and divided

2 c. cooked turkey, diced

4-oz. can diced green chiles

3 c. medium-hot salsa

salt and pepper to taste

4 c. tortilla chips, coarsely broken

2 c. shredded Mexican-blend cheese

Garnish: sour cream

In a large cast-iron skillet, heat olive oil over medium heat. Add 1-1/4 cups onion; cook until softened, about 5 minutes. Add turkey and chiles; cook for 3 minutes. Stir in salsa; simmer over low heat until heated through. Season with salt and pepper. Gently fold in tortilla chips; top with cheese. Transfer skillet to oven. Bake, uncovered, at 450 degrees for about 5 minutes, just until cheese melts. At serving time, sprinkle with remaining onion; dollop with sour cream.

Makes 4 to 6 servings.

JUST FOR FUN

Tombstone, Ruby, Gillette, and Gunsight are among the ghost towns scattered throughout Arizona.

HONEY CHICKEN & STUFFING

MARY GARCIA
PHOENIX, AZ

An all-in-one family meal that's good enough for guests! Best of all, it's easy to make ahead...prepare, tuck in the fridge and then bake just in time for dinner.

Combine stuffing, water, raisins and butter; toss to mix and let stand for 3 minutes. Spoon stuffing mixture in 6 mounds into a 13"x9" baking pan sprayed with non-stick vegetable spray. Place one chicken breast on top of each mound. Mix together remaining ingredients; spoon over chicken. Cover baking pan with aluminum foil. Bake at 400 degrees for 25 to 30 minutes. Remove foil and bake for an additional 5 minutes, or until golden.

Serves 6.

3 c. herb-flavored
  stuffing mix
1 c. hot water
1/2 c. golden raisins
2 T. butter, melted
6 boneless, skinless
  chicken breasts
1/2 c. honey
1/3 c. mayonnaise
1/3 c. Dijon mustard
1/2 t. dried parsley

ENCHILADA LASAGNA

JUDI LANCE
PAYSON, AZ

This is our family's favorite dish. The cream cheese is what really makes this dish wonderful. Pair with a crisp fresh salad, and dinner is served!

1 lb. lean ground beef

1 onion, chopped

1 green pepper, chopped

1 red pepper, chopped

8-oz. pkg. cream cheese, cubed

1 t. garlic powder

10-oz. can red enchilada sauce

6 8-inch corn tortillas

1 c. shredded Cheddar cheese, divided

Optional: sour cream, salsa

In a large skillet over medium heat, sauté beef, onion and peppers until beef is no longer pink. Drain; stir in cream cheese and garlic powder. Cook and stir until cheese is melted; remove from heat and set aside. Pour enchilada sauce into a shallow bowl. Dip 2 tortillas into sauce and place in a lightly greased 13"x9" baking pan. Spread tortillas with half the beef mixture; sprinkle with 1/3 cup shredded cheese. Repeat layers; top with remaining tortillas, sauce and cheese. Bake, uncovered, at 400 degrees for 20 to 25 minutes, until heated through and cheese is melted. Serve with sour cream and salsa, if desired.

Serves 6.

ROAST TURKEY BREAST

KIMBERLY MARLATT
YUMA, AZ

Last year, I used an electric roaster to cook our Christmas turkey... the results were wonderful! Not only did it cook much faster, but it was also moist, delicious and beautifully golden.

Remove gravy packet and giblets from turkey, if necessary, and discard. Pat turkey dry with paper towels. In a bowl, combine butter, garlic and seasonings. Add one tablespoon juice from lemon; mix well. Using your hands, loosen turkey skin from breast. Spread a few tablespoons of butter mixture under the skin and over the meat. Once you take your hands out, you can "massage" the skin to help spread the butter mixture around underneath. Spread 2 more tablespoons of butter mixture over the outer skin. Place orange and lemon halves inside the cavity. Pour broth into a roasting pan, under the rack. Place prepared turkey on the rack; cover with aluminum foil. Bake at 350 degrees for one hour. Remove foil; using a basting brush, brush remaining butter mixture over turkey. Cover; bake for one more hour, or until turkey is fully cooked and a meat thermometer reads 165 to 170 degrees when inserted into breast. Remove from roaster and let stand, covered with foil, for about 15 to 20 minutes before slicing.

8-1/2 lb. turkey breast, thawed
1/2 c. butter, softened
2 to 3 cloves garlic, minced
1 to 1-1/2 t. poultry seasoning
1/8 t. pepper
1 lemon, halved
1 orange, halved
3 c. turkey or chicken broth

Serves 6 to 8.

BAKED CHICKEN CACCIATORE

JULIE GASPARRO
SCOTTSDALE, AZ

My family's favorite dinner! I make it at least twice a month and no wonder...it's delicious and you don't even have to precook the pasta! Use your own homemade sauce or a favorite store brand.

6 boneless, skinless
  chicken breasts

3 green and/or red
  peppers, chopped

2 onions, chopped

4 cloves garlic, chopped

16-oz. pkg. penne pasta,
  uncooked

4 c. spaghetti sauce

1 c. water

8-oz. pkg. shredded
  mozzarella cheese

1/4 c. shredded
  Parmesan cheese

Arrange chicken in a well-greased 13"x9" baking pan. Arrange peppers and onions around chicken. Add uncooked pasta, pushing down around chicken and vegetables. Pour sauce evenly over all; drizzle with water. Cover completely with heavy-duty aluminum foil, sealing edges tightly around pan so no steam can escape. Bake at 350 degrees for one hour. Uncover and sprinkle with cheeses. Bake, uncovered, for another 20 to 30 minutes. Serve pasta mixture topped with chicken.

Makes 6 servings.

TOMATO-BEEF CAVATAPPI CASSEROLE

SHARON GUTIERREZ
LITCHFIELD PARK, AZ

This dish was a favorite of my two sons Ernie and Dave when they were growing up. They're now in their 30s and they still always request it when they visit. It's simple to toss together...add a crisp salad and warm bread for an easy dinner. It's great to take to a potluck too.

Cook pasta according to package directions; drain. Add pasta to a 13"x9" baking pan sprayed with non-stick vegetable spray; set aside. Brown beef in a skillet over medium heat; drain and add seasonings as desired. Stir in tomato sauce. Reduce heat to low; simmer for 10 minutes. Spoon beef mixture over pasta; stir gently to coat with sauce. Sprinkle with cheese. Cover with aluminum foil. Bake at 350 degrees for 15 to 30 minutes, until hot and bubbly. Let stand 10 minutes before serving.

Makes 8 servings.

16-oz. pkg. cavatappi pasta or elbow macaroni, uncooked

1 lb. ground beef chuck

1/2 t. onion salt or onion powder

1/2 t. garlic salt or garlic powder

Optional: salt and pepper to taste

2 8-oz. cans tomato sauce

2 c. shredded Cheddar cheese

SPICED HOLIDAY HAM

**LORA CHRISTENSEN
SNOWFLAKE, AZ**

*My husband & I were newlyweds when my mother asked us to bring
a ham for Thanksgiving. I panicked, thinking of purchasing sliced
deli ham. We asked my mother-in-law, who's a wonderful cook, for
help. She gave me this recipe that's very easy to remember and put
together. You really can't mess it up! Later, all three of my sisters
called to ask me for the recipe so they could serve this ham to their
families at Christmas.*

**10 to 12-lb. fully cooked
bone-in ham**

3 T. cinnamon

2 T. ground cloves

2 t. nutmeg

**16-oz. pkg. brown
sugar**

**30-oz. can crushed
pineapple**

Place ham in an ungreased roasting pan. Mix spices
in a small bowl; rub over ham. In a separate bowl,
mix brown sugar and pineapple with juices; spoon
over ham. Insert a meat thermometer in center of
ham without touching bone. Cover and bake at 325
degrees for 2-1/4 to 2-3/4 hours, until thermometer
reads 140 degrees. Remove ham to a serving
platter; let stand for 20 minutes before slicing.

Makes about 20 servings.

LAYERED MEXICAN PIZZAS

HELENE GIBSON
YUMA, AZ

Double-decker delights made with crisp tostada shells.

Brown ground beef in a skillet over medium heat. Drain; add seasoning mix according to package directions. You will use 2 shells for each pizza. Spread 6 shells with refried beans. Layer ground beef mixture over refried beans, top with cheese and one tablespoon sauce per shell. Place remaining shells on top; sprinkle with lettuce, tomatoes with chiles and onion. Cover with cheese and drizzle with one tablespoon sauce per shell. Place on a lightly greased baking sheet. Bake at 350 degrees for about 5 minutes, just until cheese melts.

Makes 6 servings.

1 lb. ground beef
1-1/4 oz. pkg. burrito
  seasoning mix
12 corn tostada shells
16-oz. can refried beans
8-oz. pkg. shredded
  Mexican-blend cheese
10-oz. can red enchilada
  sauce
2 c. shredded lettuce
14-1/2 oz. can diced
  tomatoes with chiles
1 onion, chopped

SLOW-COOKED HAM DINNER

ANGELA MURPHY
TEMPE, AZ

This is a wonderful, tasty slow-cooker recipe. It's a quick, easy and very filling.

Combine all ingredients into a 6-quart slow cooker. Cover and cook on low setting for 6 hours or until potatoes are tender. Once cooked, remove lid and let it cool for 20 minutes before serving.

Makes 6 to 8 servings.

6 small russet potatoes,
  peeled and diced
1 small white onion,
  diced
12-oz. pkg. fresh green
  beans
4 c. cooked boneless
  ham, cubed
10-1/2 oz. can cream of
  potato soup
1/2 c. vegetable broth
1/2 c. milk
salt and pepper to taste

TEENY'S MEXICAN CASSEROLE

ELLEN MATTINGLY
FLAGSTAFF, AZ

This is a quick recipe that my mother would feed all of us after work. Growing up in Prescott, Arizona, it was always a treat to eat this once a week at least. Then after getting married and having 3 children of my own, I have always had this on our table as well. We lived in New Orleans for 30 years, but after Hurricane Katrina, we're back in Arizona again. I hope you all will like it too!

1 to 1-1/2 lbs. ground beef

1/2 c. onion, chopped

4-oz. can chopped green chiles

3/4 t. salt-free herb seasoning

3/4 t. garlic powder

3/4 t. ground cumin

3/4 t. paprika

salt and pepper to taste

12 6-inch corn tortillas, torn into bite-size pieces

10-3/4 oz. can cream of celery or mushroom soup

1/4 c. milk

12-oz. pkg. shredded sharp or mild Cheddar cheese, divided

Cook ground beef and onion in a skillet until beef is browned and onion is tender. Drain; stir in chiles and seasonings. Place tortilla pieces in a large bowl; add soup, milk and 2 cups cheese. Spoon warm meat mixture over tortillas. Mix all very well and place in a greased 11"x7" baking pan; top with remaining cheese. Bake, uncovered, at 350 degrees for 20 to 25 minutes, until bubbly and golden on top.

Serves 4 to 6.

SUPER-EASY BBQ CHICKEN

BOBBIE SOFIA
LAKE HAVASU CITY, AZ

I've lived in the desert Southwest most of my adult life, so I know barbecue is not just for summer! So simple to fix in your slow cooker... just add a fresh green salad for a wonderful meal.

Place chicken in a microwave-safe dish. Cover and microwave on high for 15 minutes. Carefully remove hot chicken to a 6-quart slow cooker, spooning some barbecue sauce over each piece. Cover and cook on low setting for 6 to 8 hours. Discard bones. Serve chicken and sauce over rice.

Serves 6 to 8.

16 chicken drumsticks and/or thighs, skin removed

2 c. favorite barbecue sauce

cooked rice

GRANNY'S WINTER DINNER

MARTHA-ANN DALY
FLAGSTAFF, AZ

My grandmother made this simple oven stew for us on cold winter nights. It has continued to be a family favorite for many years. With a crisp green salad and a light dessert, it's a complete meal.

In a large, heavy saucepan, brown beef in shortening over medium heat. Drain; add water and mushrooms with liquid. Reduce heat to low; cover and simmer for 2 hours. Transfer beef mixture to an ungreased 13"x9" baking pan; arrange potatoes on top. In a separate bowl, mix sour cream, soup and milk; spoon over potatoes. Sprinkle cheese on top. Bake, uncovered, at 350 degrees for 1-1/2 hours.

Serves 4 to 6.

1 lb. stew beef, cubed

2 T. shortening

1 c. water

4-oz. jar button mushrooms

3 potatoes, peeled and sliced

3/4 c. sour cream

10-3/4 oz. can cream of mushroom soup

3/4 c. milk

1 c. shredded Cheddar cheese

SLOW-COOKED SPAGHETTI & PORK

GLENDA BARRICK
ROOSEVELT, AZ

When John & I were first married, he told me that spaghetti was the only dish he wouldn't eat. I really like it, so after awhile, I decided to fix it anyway. I asked him to give it a try, and if he didn't like it, I would make him something else. He took one bite and told me I could make spaghetti for him anytime! This delicious recipe is an easy way to feed a crowd. Just add garlic toast and a tossed salad.

4 lbs. country-style pork ribs, cut into serving-size pieces

garlic salt and pepper to taste

7-oz. jar pasta sauce

14-1/2 oz. can diced tomatoes

6-oz. can tomato paste

1 c. Lambrusco or Zinfandel wine or water

1 onion, chopped

1/4 c. grated Parmesan cheese

1 T. garlic, minced, or more to taste

1 t. Italian seasoning

1/2 t. sugar

1 to 2 16-oz. pkgs. spaghetti, cooked

Garnish: additional grated Parmesan cheese, red pepper flakes

Season ribs with garlic salt and pepper; arrange in a large slow cooker. Add remaining ingredients except spaghetti and garnish; stir together. Cover and cook on low setting for 8 hours, or until ribs are very tender. Remove ribs from sauce; arrange on a serving platter. To serve, either place cooked spaghetti on dinner plates and top with sauce, or add sauce to the drained spaghetti in its pot, toss to mix and transfer to a serving bowl. Garnish with additional Parmesan cheese and red pepper flakes.

Serves 8 to 10.

Arizona

DEB'S CASHEW CHICKEN

**DEBBIE DEVERILL
GILBERT, AZ**

I was house-sitting for some dear friends and wanted to have supper ready for them when they got home. My family loves this recipe, so I made it for my friends and they loved it too. Fix some white or brown rice, and dinner is ready.

In a 6-quart slow cooker, combine all ingredients except chicken, cashews and rice; stir. Add chicken; push into soup mixture. Cover and cook on low setting for 4 to 6 hours, or on high setting for 2 to 3 hours, until chicken is cooked through. Stir in cashews just before serving. Serve chicken and vegetable mixture over cooked rice.

Makes 4 to 6 servings.

10-3/4 oz. can cream of mushroom or chicken soup

1 lb. fresh bean sprouts, or 14-oz. can bean sprouts, drained

1 c. celery, sliced

4-oz. can sliced mushrooms, drained

1/2 c. green onions, chopped

3 T. butter, sliced

1 T. soy sauce

4 to 6 boneless, skinless chicken breasts

1 c. whole cashews

cooked rice

LAZY LASAGNA

DONNA HENRICKS
MESA, AZ

*When we lived in Ohio, we had neighborhood parties often. This was
one of our favorites from those days...it still is. Can't stay out of it...
even a spoonful cold from the fridge is yummy!*

8-oz. pkg. medium egg
noodles, uncooked

1-1/2 lbs. ground beef
seasoning

salt to taste

8-oz. pkg. cream cheese,
cubed

1 c. cottage cheese

1 c. sour cream

15-oz. can tomato sauce

Garnish: grated
Parmesan cheese

Cook noodles according to package directions; drain.
Meanwhile, in a large skillet over medium heat,
brown beef. Drain; sprinkle to taste with seasoning
salt. Combine beef and noodles with remaining
ingredients except Parmesan cheese. Transfer to a
lightly greased deep 13"x9" baking pan; sprinkle with
Parmesan cheese. Bake, uncovered, at 375 degrees
for 45 minutes. Let stand for a few minutes before
serving.

Makes 8 to 10 servings.

RANCHO GRANDE CASEROLE

MONICA CANTRELL
TAYLOR, AZ

This recipe is from my aunt...it's great for feeding a crowd!

In a large skillet, lightly brown beef with onions and green pepper; drain. Stir in tomato sauce, kidney beans, rice, chili powder and salt. Spoon into a lightly greased 13"x9" baking pan. Bake, covered, at 350 degrees for 40 minutes. Remove from oven and arrange tamales on top of casserole. Spoon chili sauce from tamales over top; sprinkle with cheese. Return to oven and continue baking, uncovered, 20 minutes longer. Garnish with sliced olives.

Makes 12 servings.

1-1/2 lbs. lean ground beef
2 onions, chopped
1 green pepper, chopped
3 8-oz. cans tomato sauce
2 16-oz. can kidney beans, drained and rinsed
2 c. cooked rice
2 t. chili powder
1-1/2 t. salt
2 15-oz. cans tamales
1 c. shredded Cheddar cheese
Garnish: 2-1/4 oz. can sliced black olives, drained

CAROL'S CHEESE ENCHILADAS

CAROL THOMPSON
CASA GRANDE, AZ

This has become one of my children's favorite recipes. They requested it often when they were growing up. They never realized that I gradually tweaked it over the years to make it healthier!

8-oz. container low-fat sour cream

8-oz. pkg. low-fat cream cheese, softened

8-oz. pkg. low-fat shredded Cheddar cheese

1/2 c. onion, diced

4-oz. can chopped green chiles

10 8-inch flour tortillas

20-oz. can red or green enchilada sauce

In a large bowl, combine all ingredients except tortillas and enchilada sauce; mix well. Place 1/4 cup of mixture on the edge of each tortilla; roll up tightly. Spray a 13"x9" baking pan with non-stick vegetable spray. Place filled tortillas in pan, seam-side down. Spoon sauce over tortillas. Bake, covered, at 350 degrees for 25 to 30 minutes.

Makes 10 servings.

KITCHEN TIP

When prepping for a recipe, see which ingredients are added together and combine them ahead of time.

CHRISTMAS SHEPHERD'S PIE

**MARLA KINNERSLEY
SURPRISE, AZ**

*This is comfort food at its finest! It's so easy to make...perfect to
serve in the holiday season because of the red and green colors.
We really like it on Christmas Eve with a side salad. I hope your
family enjoys it as much as we do!*

In a skillet over medium heat, cook beef with onion
until beef is no longer pink; drain. Stir in garlic
powder, tomato soup and green beans. Spoon
beef mixture into a lightly greased 13"x9" baking
pan. Prepare potato flakes according to package
directions; spread over beef mixture. Top with
cheese. Bake, uncovered, at 350 degrees for 30
minutes. Let stand for 10 minutes before serving.

Makes 8 servings.

1 lb. ground beef
3/4 c. yellow onion, diced
1 t. garlic powder
10-1/2 oz. can tomato
  soup
2 14-1/2 oz. cans green
  beans, drained
8-oz. pkg. instant
  mashed potato flakes
8-oz. pkg. shredded
  Cheddar cheese

CHAPTER FIVE

A-TO-Z

Appetizers & Snacks

**PERFECT FOR PLANNING FOR
COMPANY OR WHEN YOU'RE IN
NEED OF A LITTLE SNACK...THESE
RECIPES ARE GREAT FOR TAKING
ON-THE-GO OR AS A PRE-DINNER
PLEASER FOR YOUR GUESTS**

PROSCIUTTO-WRAPPED ASPARAGUS

ANN TOBER
BISCOE, AZ

*This simple and pretty presentation of asparagus is always a hit
at any party or event.*

**1 bunch asparagus,
about 10 pieces,
trimmed**

1 T. olive oil

1 t. kosher salt

1 t. pepper

**3-oz. pkg. sliced
prosciutto, cut into
strips with fat
removed**

Optional: lemon slices

Toss asparagus with oil, salt and pepper. Arrange in a single layer on an ungreased rimmed baking sheet. Bake at 400 degrees for 5 minutes. Allow to cool slightly. Wrap each asparagus spear with a strip of prosciutto. Return to oven and bake for 4 more minutes, or until asparagus is crisp-tender and prosciutto is slightly browned. Serve warm or at room temperature, garnished with thin lemon slices, if desired.

Serves 6.

WARM SEAFOOD DIP

CAROL AGUILAR
TUCSON, AZ

*During the holidays, I like to use the multi-colored tortilla chips for dipping
to make it more festive!*

**2 8-oz. pkgs. cream
cheese, cubed**

1/2 lb. tiny shrimp

**1/4 lb. imitation
crabmeat, flaked**

1 T. lemon juice

**1 t. Worcestershire
sauce**

**1 t. garlic, minced
tortilla chips**

Combine all ingredients except tortilla chips in a slow cooker. Cover and cook on high setting for 30 minutes, or until cheese melts; stir. Turn slow cooker to low setting; cover and cook for one hour. Stir again. Serve warm with tortilla chips.

Makes 15 servings.

FRIED CHEESE STICKS

ANGELA MURPHY
TEMPE, AZ

Way better than store-bought, these are the first to go at get-togethers!

Cut cheese crosswise into 3/4 inch slices. Lay slices flat and cut in half lengwhise. Combine flour and red pepper; stir well. Combine bread crumbs and parsley in another bowl, stir well. Dip cheese sticks in beaten eggs. Dredge in flour mixture. Dip coated cheese in egg again, dredge in bread crumb mixture, pressing firmly so that crumbs adhere. Place cheese sticks on a wax paper-lined baking sheet and freeze at least 30 minutes. Fry cheese sticks in 375 degree deep oil until golden brown. Drain on paper towels. Serve immediately with marinara sauce.

Makes 28 appetizers.

2 8-oz. pkg's. Monterey Jack cheese with jalapeño peppers
1 c. all-purpose flour
1-1/2 t. ground red pepper
1 c. fine, dry bread crumbs
1 t. dried parsley
4 eggs, beaten
vegetable oil
Optional: marinara sauce

JUST FOR FUN

The amount of copper on the roof of the Arizona State Capitol building is equivalent to 4,800,000 pennies.

NONIE'S PERFECT PARTY MIX

DONNA REID
PAYSON, AZ

My mom used to make this party mix during the holidays. It was one of several treats she always had on her table for us to munch on. Now that Mom's gone, I make it and think of her.

4 c. doughnut-shaped oat cereal

2 c. bite-size crispy rice cereal squares

2 c. bite-size crispy wheat cereal squares

3 c. pretzel sticks

13-oz. container salted peanuts

1-1/2 c. walnuts, broken

1 t. celery salt

1 t. garlic salt

2 T. grated Parmesan cheese

1/4 c. butter, melted

Combine cereals, pretzels, nuts, seasonings and cheese in a slow cooker. Drizzle melted butter over cereal mixture; stir to coat well. Cover and cook on low setting for 3 to 3-1/2 hours. Remove lid and cook on low setting for 30 minutes more. Store in an airtight container.

Makes about 14 cups.

HOT CRACKERS

SCOOTER PUGH
EL DORADO, AZ

An oldie but goodie with a peppery new taste...perfect for munching!

16-oz. pkg. saltine crackers

1/2 t. garlic powder

1 T. red pepper flakes

1-1/3 c. canola oil

1-oz. pkg. dry ranch salad dressing mix

Place crackers in a gallon glass jar with a tight-fitting lid. Mix together remaining ingredients and pour over crackers. Turn jar on its side; roll until crackers are well coated. Let stand 2 to 3 hours, then break apart and store in an airtight container.

Makes about one pound.

JJ'S BEER MEATBALLS

JANINE JACKSON
PAGE, AZ

I have made these meatballs for over 40 years, and never had a bad review. You can't eat just one! They taste a bit like sweet-and-sour meatballs. I have to double or triple this recipe for my family. It is very good served over pasta too.

Roll beef into one-inch balls; add to a large skillet over medium heat. Brown on all sides; drain well and set aside. If using frozen meatballs; omit this step; simply thaw. In a Dutch oven over medium heat, combine catsup, beer and sugar. Cook and stir until sugar is dissolved. Add meatballs; reduce heat to low. Cover and simmer for 30 to 40 minutes, stirring occasionally, until sauce thickens. Transfer meatballs with sauce to a serving bowl. Serve with small plates and a container of toothpicks.

2 lbs. lean ground beef, or 32-oz. pkg. frozen homestyle meatballs

14-oz. bottle catsup

12-oz. can regular or non-alcoholic beer

1 c. sugar

Makes 8 to 12 servings.

JUST FOR FUN

In 1869 Grand Canyon's Disaster Falls was named to commemorate the site of an expedition boat wreck. The boat called "No Name," was destroyed in the rapids during a three-month voyage down the Green and Colorado Rivers and then into the unknown depts of the Grand Canyon.

MARLA'S GOOD SALSA

**MARLA KINNERSLEY
SURPRISE, AZ**

A favorite in our home...there's just something about this salsa that keeps everyone coming back for more. We really enjoy it with lime-flavored tortilla chips!

**28-oz. can crushed
  tomatoes
3 T. fresh cilantro,
  chopped
2 t. canned pickled
  jalapeño peppers,
  minced
1/2 t. garlic powder
1/2 t. ground cumin
1/4 t. salt**

In a serving bowl, combine tomatoes with juice and remaining ingredients; mix well. Cover and chill for at least one hour before serving.

Serves 4.

EASY CREAMY ARTICHOKE DIP

**MARY GARCIA
PHOENIX, AZ**

So delicious, I usually have to make a second batch!

**14-oz. can artichoke
  hearts, drained and
  squeezed dry
1/2 c. mayonnaise
1/4 c. grated Parmesan
  cheese
1 clove garlic, minced
Garnish: paprika
assorted crackers**

In a bowl, mash artichokes. Stir in mayonnaise, cheese and garlic. Cover and chill. At serving time, sprinkle with paprika. Serve with crackers.

Serves 6.

BAKED ZUCCHINI STICKS

CYNTHIA DODGE
QUEEN CREEK, AZ

This is a quick and nutritious way to get your family to eat more vegetables. Plus, it's a good way to use up all of that zucchini your neighbors leave on your doorstep! Works great with yellow summer squash also.

Cut zucchini into sticks, 2 to 3 inches long and about 1/4-inch thick; set aside. In a large bowl, mix together bread crumbs and spices; set aside. In a separate bowl, beat egg whites with an electric mixer on high setting until soft peaks form. Roll zucchini sticks in egg whites to coat well. Roll sticks into bread crumb mixture; place on lightly greased baking sheets. Bake at 425 degrees for 8 to 10 minutes, until lightly golden. Serve warm with a favorite dipping sauce or salad dressing.

3 small to medium
  zucchini, ends trimmed
1 c. Italian-flavored dry
  bread crumbs
1/4 t. garlic powder
1/4 t. onion powder
2 egg whites, beaten
Garnish: ranch salad
  dressing

Makes 8 servings.

SOMBRERO BITES

KAREN DAVIS
GLENDALE, AZ

These crisp shells are a good container for crab dip too.

Brown beed and set aside. Spray 24 mini muffin cups with non-stick vegetable spray; press a wonton wrapper into each cup. Bake at 350 degrees for 10 minutes, until crisp. Mix together corn, beans, beef and salsa; spoon into cups. Top with cheese and sour cream.

24 wonton wrappers
1 lb. ground beef,
  browned and drained
15-1/4 oz. can corn,
  drained
16-oz. can black beans,
  drained and rinsed
8-oz. jar salsa
Garnish: Cheddar
  cheese and sour cream

Makes 2 dozen.

HOLIDAY GUACAMOLE

**MARLA KINNERSLEY
SURPRISE, AZ**

*My friend of 30 years, Jen, shared a simpler version of this recipe with
me. I have played around with the recipe until it became this amazing
holiday guacamole, which gets eaten up every single time it's put out.
Everyone wants to know what's in it, because it's so darn good! If you
can find red and green tortilla chips, arrange them around the bowl to
look like a festive wreath. Enjoy!*

**3 ripe avocados, peeled,
pitted and diced**

**1-1/2 c. seedless red
grapes, quartered**

1 c. pomegranate seeds

**1 jalapeño pepper,
seeded and minced**

**3 T. fresh cilantro,
chopped**

3 T. red onion, diced

2 cloves garlic, minced

juice of 1 lime

1/2 t. salt

1/8 t. pepper

tortilla chips

In a large bowl, mash avocado with a fork to desired
texture. Add remaining ingredients except tortilla
chips; mix well. Transfer to a festive serving bowl;
serve with your favorite tortilla chips around it.

Makes 8 servings.

PARTY-PLEASING FIESTA DIP

CHRISTINE TAYLOR
SURRISE, AZ

My family & friends love this dip! Every time we have a party, it is gone fast. I also get requests to bring this to functions. The secret ingredient that no one can place is the mayonnaise. This dip is so good that my family, who hate mayonnaise, make an exception for this easy-to-make, crowd-pleasing dip because it is that great.

In a small bowl, combine sour cream, mayonnaise and taco seasoning. Mix well; cover and refrigerate at least one hour. At serving time, spread refried beans almost to the edges of a large serving platter; spread sour cream mixture over beans. Top with tomatoes, onions, olives and cheese. Serve immediately with tortilla chips.

Serves 20.

8-oz. container sour cream
1/2 c. mayonnaise
1-1/4 oz. pkg. taco seasoning mix
2 16-oz. cans refried beans
3 tomatoes, chopped
1 bunch green onions, chopped
4-oz. can sliced black olives, drained
8-oz. pkg. shredded Cheddar cheese
tortilla chips

PRESENTATION

Scattering small framed pictures of family & friends throughout your buffet table is sure to bring a smile to your guests' faces.

SO-GOOD TERIYAKI WINGS

KAREN DAVIS
GLENDALE, AZ

An oldie, but goodie...this recipe is still finger-lickin' good!

3 lbs. chicken wings,
  separated
1/3 c. lemon juice
1/4 c. catsup
1/4 c. soy sauce
1/4 c. oil
2 T. brown sugar,
  packed
1/4 t. garlic powder
1/4 t. pepper

Place chicken wings in a large plastic zipping bag; set aside. Combine remaining ingredients in a bowl. Mix well; pour over wings. Seal bag and refrigerate overnight, turning bag occasionally. Arrange wings on a wire rack in a greased shallow 15"x10" jelly-roll pan. Bake at 375 degrees for 40 to 45 minutes, turning and basting several times with pan juices, until golden and chicken juices run clear.

Makes 2 to 3 dozen.

ARIZONA CHEESE CRISPS

MARY COKER
APACHE JUNCTION, AZ

This is a southwestern favorite at many local Mexican restaurants.

2 large flour tortillas
8-oz. pkg. shredded
  Cheddar or Mexican-
  blend cheese
2 t. butter, softened

Line 2 pizza pans or baking sheets with aluminum foil; spray foil with non-stick vegetable spray and set aside. Spread each tortilla with one teaspoon softened butter; place on pans. Bake at 400 degrees for 3 to 5 minutes, until tortillas are crisp and lightly golden. Remove from oven; evenly spread each tortilla with one cup cheese. Return to oven until cheese is melted. Cut with a pizza cutter or knife into 12 pieces.

Serves 6, 2 pieces each.

ZESTY CHILI DIP

ROSALYN SMITH
APACHE JUNCTION, AZ

My husband shared this dip recipe with me at our first camping experience as a new family. It's speedy to make and hearty enough to be a meal. I'm sure you will like it too!

Brown beef in a skillet over medium heat; drain. Add cheese and chili to skillet; reduce heat. Simmer for about 10 minutes, stirring occasionally, until cheese is melted. Serve warm with tortilla chips.

Serves 5 to 10.

1 lb. ground beef
16-oz. pkg. Mexican pasteurized process cheese spread, cubed
15-oz. can hot chili with beans
15-oz. can chili with no beans
tortilla chips

BACON-PARMESAN DIP

RENEE WALSTON
PEORIA, AZ

My hubby John loves to create in the kitchen...he is an artist when it comes to mixing ingredients! This is just one of his many recipes. It's delicious with chips, crackers and veggies.

In a skillet over medium heat, cook bacon until crisp; drain and crumble. Combine bacon, cheese, onion, garlic and pepper in a food processor. Pulse until all ingredients are finely chopped; transfer to a bowl. Add sour cream and mayonnaise; stir until well combined. Cover and chill for at least an hour.

Makes about 2 cups.

4 slices bacon
2/3 c. grated Parmesan cheese
1/4 onion, sliced
1 clove garlic
1 t. coarse pepper
8-oz. container sour cream
2 T. mayonnaise

BUFFALO CHICKEN PINWHEELS

JO ANN
GOOSEBERRY PATCH

Tortilla pinwheels are a favorite of ours for parties. So easy to make...so good to eat! I like to use different colors of tortillas for a little variety.

- 2 8-oz. pkgs. cream cheese, softened
- 1-oz. pkg. ranch salad dressing mix
- 1/2 c. buffalo wing sauce
- 1 c. shredded Cheddar cheese
- 1 c. green onions, chopped
- 1-1/2 c. cooked chicken, shredded, or 2 5-oz. cans chicken, drained and flaked
- 6 10-inch flour tortillas
- Garnish: ranch or blue cheese salad dressing

Combine cream cheese and salad dressing mix in a large bowl. Beat with an electric mixer on medium speed until well blended; beat in wing sauce. Stir in cheese, onions and chicken. Spread mixture evenly over tortillas. Roll up tightly; cover with plastic and chill for 3 hours. Cut into one-inch slices, fasten with toothpicks, if desired. Serve with salad dressing for dipping.

Makes about 5 dozen.

POOR MAN'S APPETIZER

TRACY NEEDHAM
SAN TAN VALLEY, AZ

This is the very first appetizer my mom taught me to make. It's suitable for any occasion and will please just about anyone.

- 1 c. mayonnaise
- 3 T. grated Parmesan cheese
- 1/4 c. red onion, chopped
- 1 baguette, sliced 1/4-inch thick

In a bowl, mix mayonnaise, onion and cheese. Spread mixture onto baguette slices; place on an ungreased baking sheet. Turn oven broiler to high with rack set 2 slots down. Broil until tops are golden and bubbly. Remove from baking sheet; allow to cool slightly before serving.

Serves 6 to 8.

Arizona

QUILTERS' SQUARES

DOLORES BROCK
WELLTON, AZ

My friend Helen shared this recipe with me...she would always prepare it for our quilters' meetings. Now, whenever I make it, I think of her and the sweet little hat she always wore.

Brown beef, pork and onion in a skillet over medium heat; drain. Add remaining ingredients except rye slices. Cook and stir until cheese is melted. Arrange rye slices on an ungreased baking sheet. Spread each with one tablespoon beef mixture. Bake at 450 degrees for 8 minutes, or until bubbly.

Makes 3 dozen.

1 lb. ground beef

1 lb. ground pork sausage

1 onion, chopped

16-oz. pkg. pasteurized process cheese spread, cubed

1 T. Worcestershire sauce

1/2 t. garlic salt

1/2 t. dried oregano

2 T. fresh parsley, minced

1 loaf sliced party rye

CHEESY POTATO SKINS

DOLORES BROCK
WELLTON, AZ

We love to dip these potato skins in ranch dressing.

Place potatoes on a baking sheet; sprinkle with cheeses. Top with onions and bacon; heat under broiler until cheese melts.

Serves 4.

4 potatoes, baked and halved

1/2 c. shredded Cheddar cheese

1/2 c. shredded mozzarella cheese

2 green onions, chopped

4 t. bacon bits

CHAPTER SIX

PAINTED DESERT

Desserts

THERE IS ALWAYS ROOM FOR
DESSERT. SO WHEN YOUR SWEET
TOOTH IS CALLING, THESE SIMPLE
SWEETS ARE THE PERFECT WAY TO
END THE DAY.

TRIPLE-LAYERED BROWNIES

**ALICIA ALLEN
LAKESIDE, AZ**

*I make these cake-type brownies for any get-together. Everyone begs for
the recipe! Be sure to use creamy frosting instead of whipped.*

20-oz. pkg. brownie mix
3 eggs, beaten
1/4 c. water
1/2 c. oil
16-oz. container cream
cheese frosting
1 c. creamy peanut
butter
12-oz. pkg. milk
chocolate chips
2-1/2 c. crispy rice cereal

In a large bowl, stir dry brownie mix, eggs, water
and oil just until combined. Grease the bottom of a
13"x9" glass baking pan; pour in batter. Bake at 350
degrees for 27 to 30 minutes. Cool in pan. Spread
frosting over cooled brownies; refrigerate until set.
In a saucepan, melt peanut butter and chocolate
chips together over low heat, stirring frequently
until smooth. Remove from heat. Mix in cereal and
spread evenly over frosting. Refrigerate until set.
Cut into squares.

Makes 2 dozen.

CARAMEL FUDGE BROWNIES

**SUE ROBERSON
PEORIA, AZ**

*This recipe came from my very special mother-in-law, and although she's
no longer with us, her recipe continues to be a family favorite.*

18-1/2 oz. pkg. German
chocolate cake mix
3/4 c. butter, melted
5-oz. can evaporated
milk, divided
14-oz. pkg. caramels,
unwrapped
1 c. semi-sweet chocolate
chips

Combine dry cake mix, butter and 1/3 cup
evaporated milk. Spread half of batter into a
greased 13"x9" baking pan (this layer will be
very thin). Bake at 350 degrees for 12 minutes.
Immediately after removing from oven, sprinkle
brownies with chocolate chips. While crust is baking,
melt caramels and remaining evaporated milk in a
microwave-safe bowl for 3 minutes on high setting.
Stir caramel mixture and pour over brownies. Spoon
remaining cake batter by heaping tablespoonfuls
over brownies; do not mix. Bake at 350 degrees for
15 to 17 minutes.

Makes 2 dozen.

Arizona

SUPER BERRY CRISP

**SANDY WIDDOWS
TUCSON, AZ**

I made this recipe one day with only the ingredients I had on hand. It turned out to be one of my husband's favorites...now I make it all the time!

Pour pie filling into an ungreased 9" pie plate; fold in blueberries. Melt butter in a small saucepan over medium-low heat. Add remaining ingredients except garnish to melted butter, stirring to coat well. Spread oat mixture over fruit in pie plate. Bake at 350 degrees for 35 minutes, or until topping is crisp and golden. Garnish individual servings with whipped cream.

Serves 8.

21-oz. can cherry pie
   filling
2 c. fresh blueberries
1/4 c. butter
1/3 c. long-cooking oats,
   uncooked
1/3 c. all-purpose flour
1/4 c. brown sugar,
   packed
1 t. sugar
1/4 t. cinnamon
Garnish: whipped cream

PRESENTATION

Drizzle melted candy melting chips on wax paper and allow it to cool. Then peel the chocolate off the paper and use it to top any iced cupcake or cake.

FESTIVE PUMPKIN BREAD PUDDING

DONNA REID
PAYSON, AZ

My family loves this bread pudding during autumn and into the Christmas season. I use pumpkins from my garden to make pumpkin purée and the flavor is amazing!

3 eggs
1-1/2 c. milk
1 c. canned pumpkin
3/4 c. brown sugar, packed
2 t. vanilla extract
1 t. cinnamon
1/2 t. nutmeg
1/4 t. ground cloves
1/2 t. salt
1 loaf brioche bread, cut into 1-inch cubes
1/2 c. golden raisins
1 T. butter
Garnish: whipped cream or vanilla ice cream

In a bowl, combine eggs, milk, pumpkin, brown sugar, vanilla, spices and salt. Whisk until smooth; set aside. In a separate bowl, toss bread cubes with raisins. Spread butter inside a slow cooker; transfer bread mixture to slow cooker. Pour milk mixture evenly over bread mixture, pressing down so bread will soak up the liquid. Cover and cook on high setting for 2 to 2-1/2 hours, until set and top is golden and puffy. Serve warm or at room temperature, garnished with whipped cream or vanilla ice cream.

Serves 6.

PRESENTATION

For an easy and fun sundae bar, pre-scoop ice cream into cupcake liners and freeze until ready to serve.

FABULOUS FUDGE PIE

STACEY KAMPE
TEMPE, AZ

This recipe was passed down from several generations...it's too yummy to keep to myself!

In a large bowl, combine flour, sugar and nuts; mix in eggs and vanilla. Add melted butter and chocolate; stir until smooth. Pour mixture into a 9" deep-dish pie plate. Bake at 325 degrees for 25 minutes, or until edges look dry. Center of pie will still be soft. Allow to cool for 15 to 20 minutes; cut into wedges.

Serves 8.

1 c. minus 1 T. all-purpose flour
1 c. sugar
1/2 c. chopped walnuts
2 eggs, lightly beaten
1 T. vanilla extract
1/2 c. butter, melted
1 sq. unsweetened baking chocolate, melted

ANNA'S YUMMY PRALINES

LINDA SMITH
FOUNTAIN HILLS, AZ

These pralines were one of our favorite candies that our grandmother would make for us at holiday time. We always looked forward to their wonderful taste. Grandma has passed on, but we still keep the tradition alive and make these at holiday time.

Combine all ingredients in a microwave-safe 4-quart glass bowl. Microwave on high heat for 12 minutes, stirring every 3 minutes. Beat mixture vigorously by hand, until sticky. Drop mixture by teaspoonfuls onto buttered wax paper; cool until firm.

Makes 3 dozen.

2 c. pecan halves
1 c. sugar
1 c. brown sugar, packed
3/4 c. evaporated milk
2 T. butter
1/8 t. salt

MOTHER-DAUGHTER OATMEAL-RAISIN COOKIES

SHERRY SHEEHAN
PHOENIX, AZ

My mom always made the best oatmeal-raisin cookies. I think she used the recipe from the back of the oatmeal box. When going through her cookbook from the early 1950s, I found her vintage recipe. I made a few changes using updated ingredients and methods. They still taste like the ones she made when I was a child! I think she would have been pleased with my changes.

1 c. butter-flavored shortening
1 c. light brown sugar, packed
1 c. sugar
2 eggs, beaten
1 t. vanilla extract
1-1/2 c. all-purpose flour
1 t. baking soda
1 t. salt
1/2 t. cinnamon
3 c. old-fashioned oats, uncooked
Optional: 1/2 c. raisins, 1/2 c. chopped walnuts

In a large bowl, blend shortening and sugars. Add eggs and vanilla; beat well. Add flour, baking soda, salt and cinnamon; mix well. Stir in oats; add raisins and/or nuts, if desired. With a cookie scoop, add dough to parchment paper-lined baking sheets, using 2 tablespoons dough per cookie. Bake at 350 degrees for 12 to 15 minutes, until golden. Let cool for several minutes; remove cookies to a wire rack to finish cooling.

Makes 3 dozen.

FROSTED PUMPKIN COOKIES

SUE HAYNES
SCOTTSDALE, AZ

This recipe has been in my family for over 30 years. My grandkids request these cookies and say that they're their favorite!

In a large bowl, mix together sugar, pumpkin and butter. Stir in remaining ingredients. Drop dough by teaspoonfuls onto ungreased baking sheets. Bake at 375 degrees for 8 to 10 minutes, until lightly golden. Immediately remove cookies to a wire rack; cool. Spread with Light Brown Glaze while glaze is still warm.

Makes 2-1/2 dozen.

Light Brown Glaze:
In a sucepan over medium heat; cook butter until delicately brown. Stir in powdered sugar and vanilla. Add milk and stir until smooth.

1 c. sugar
1 o. canned pumpkin
1/2 c. butter, softened
2 c. all-purpose flour
1 t. baking powder
1 t. baking soda
2-1/2 t. cinnamon
1/4 t. salt

LIGHT BROWN GLAZE
1/4 c. butter
1 t. vanilla extract
2 c. powdered sugar
2 T. milk

PUMPKIN-OAT SCOTCHIES

STEFANIE FIERRO ARMS
GILBERT, AZ

I have been enjoying this recipe for years! It really gets a cozy
fall day off to a good start here in Arizona.

2 c. old-fashioned oats,
  uncooked
1 c. all-purpose flour
3/4 c. brown sugar,
  packed
1/2 c. butterscotch chips
1 t. baking soda
1/2 t. salt
1/2 t. pumpkin pie spice
1/2 t. cinnamon
3/4 c. butter, softened
1/2 c. sugar
1 egg, beaten
1/2 c. canned pumpkin
1 t. vanilla extract

In a bowl, combine oats, flour, brown sugar,
butterscotch chips, baking soda, salt and spices.
Mix well and set aside. In a large bowl, blend butter
and sugar together. Add egg, pumpkin and vanilla;
stir well. Add oat mixture to butter mixture; mix
well. Scoop dough into one-inch balls. Place on
ungreased baking sheets, 2 inches apart. Bake at
350 degrees for 10 minutes. Cool on wire racks.

Makes 3 dozen.

BLUE-RIBBON PECAN PIE

GAIL KELSEY
PHOENIX, AZ

*This pie has won a blue ribbon at our state fair every time I entered it! It's
a family favorite and is always a part of our Christmas dinner.*

9-inch pie crust,
  unbaked
1/2 c. pecan halves
3 eggs
1 c. dark corn syrup
1 c. sugar
1 t. vanilla extract
1/8 t. salt

Place unbaked crust in a 9" pie plate. Arrange
pecans in crust; set aside. In a bowl, beat eggs well.
Add remaining ingredients; mix well. Pour mixture
over pecans in crust. Bake at 400 degrees for 15
minutes; reduce oven to 325 degrees. Bake an
additional 30 minutes, or until center of pie is set.
Cool completely.

Serves 8.

APPLE SLICE BARS

**SUE ROBERSON-HAYNES
SCOTTSDALE, AZ**

*This recipe is so much fun to make! It's a favorite of mine that
brings back memories of great times with great family & friends
back in Wausau, Wisconsin.*

Arrange 2 pie crusts side-by-side on an ungreased
15"x10" jelly-roll pan; press seam together. Spread
crushed cereal over crusts; set aside. In a bowl,
toss apples with sugar and cinnamon. Spread apple
mixture evenly over cereal. Top with remaining 2
pie crusts; pinch edges together to seal. In a small
bowl, beat egg white with an electric mixer on high
until stiff peaks form; brush over crust. Bake at 350
degrees for 30 to 35 minutes. Cool slightly. Combine
remaining ingredients; stir to a drizzling consistency
and drizzle over crust. Cut into bars. Serve warm or
cooled.

Makes 2 dozen.

2 14-oz. pkgs.
  refrigerated pie crusts,
  unbaked and divided
1 c. corn flake cereal,
  crushed
5 c. tart apples, peeled,
  cored and cut into bite-
  sized chunks
1-1/2 c. sugar
1 t. cinnamon, or more
  to taste
1 egg white
1 c. powdered sugar
2 T. lemon juice
1/8 t. white vinegar

JUST FOR FUN

**The first woman to become justice of
the US Supreme Court, Sandra Day
O'Connor, spent her childhood on her
family's ranch in Arizona. A college
of law at Arizona State University in
Phoenix honors her legacy.**

WONDERFUL WACKY CAKE

SUSAN ROBINSON
ELGIN, AZ

When my kids were young, they helped me make this chocolate cake...a delicious homemade dessert in less than an hour.

3 c. all-purpose flour
2 c. sugar
6 T. baking cocoa
2 t. baking soda
1 t. salt
2 c. water
3/4 c. oil
2 t. vanilla extract
2 T. vinegar
Optional: frosting

Sift together flour, sugar, cocoa, baking soda and salt into a large bowl. Add remaining ingredients except frosting; mix until smooth. Pour into a lightly greased 13"x9" baking pan. Bake at 350 degrees for 30 to 35 minutes. Cool; frost if desired.

Makes 10 servings.

HELEN'S LEMON BARS

CAROL GRAY
PEORIA, AZ

I am a snowbird here in Arizona and got this recipe from my neighbor Helen, who makes the best lemon bars. Everyone loves them! We have a lot of lemon trees in our neighborhood and this is a great way to enjoy using the lemon juice.

2-1/4 c. all-purpose flour, divided
1/2 c. powdered sugar
1 c. butter
4 eggs
2 c. sugar
1/3 c. lemon juice
1/2 t. baking powder
Garnish: additional powdered sugar

In a bowl, sift together 2 cups flour and powdered sugar. Cut in butter until mixture clings together. Press into the bottom of a lightly greased 11"x9" baking pan. Bake at 350 degrees for 20 to 25 minutes; set aside. Beat eggs in another bowl; beat in sugar and lemon juice. Stir in remaining flour and baking powder; pour over baked crust. Return to oven for 25 minutes. Remove from oven; sprinkle with additional powdered sugar. Cool. Cut into 2-inch bars.

Makes 20 bars.

 Arizona -- -- -- -- --

PISTACHIO BUNDT CAKE

FAYE MAYBERRY
SAINT DAVID, AZ

This is a quick & easy cake and so unique because of the light green color. The recipe was given to me by a friend who makes it for her grandchildren. They love the green color! Now I make it for my grandchildren and they love it too. It doesn't need any frosting, it is so moist and perfect. Sometimes I will dust it with a little powdered sugar when taking to a potluck.

Combine dry cake and pudding mixes in a bowl; add remaining ingredients. Beat only until moistened; a few lumps may remain. Pour batter into a greased and floured Bundt® pan. Bake at 350 degrees for 40 to 50 minutes. Do not overbake. Cool for 10 minutes before turning cake out of pan.

Makes 12 servings.

15-1/4 oz. pkg. yellow cake mix

3-oz. pkg instant pistachio pudding mix

3/4 c. coconut oil or canola oil

4 eggs, beaten

1 t. almond extract

8-oz. container sour cream or Greek yogurt

MOM'S KRAZY KAKE

BARBARA TAYLOR
PRESCOTT VALLEY, AZ

Back in the 1950s, my mom came up with lots of recipes to feed the four of us hungry kids. This was a favorite dessert of ours and now I've passed this recipe down to my granddaughter with my mother's memory in mind.

1-1/2 c. all-purpose flour
1 c. sugar
3 T. baking cocoa
1 t. baking soda
1 t. salt
6 T. oil
1 T. cider vinegar
1 t. vanilla extract
1 c. cold water
Garnish: powdered
   sugar

Sift together flour, sugar, baking cocoa, baking soda and salt. Spoon into a parchment paper-lined 8"x8" baking pan. With a spoon, make 3 wells in dry ingredients. Pour oil into first well, vinegar into second well and vanilla into third well. Pour water over top; mix gently. Bake at 350 degrees for 30 minutes. Cool; cut into squares and dust with powdered sugar.

Makes 8 servings.

COUNTRY BUTTERMILK PIE

DONNA TURNER
QUEEN CREEK, AZ

This was my father's favorite pie. It's a little old-fashioned and unusual... we love it. It is still very popular in Texas, where my family and I were born and raised.

3 c. sugar
3 T. all-purpose flour
3 eggs
1 c. buttermilk
1/2 c. butter, melted
1 t. vanilla extract
   Option:
1 t. lemon extract
9-inch pie crust

Mix sugar and flour together; beat eggs well and add to sugar mixture. Blend in remaining ingredients except crust. Pour into pie crust. Bake at 350 degrees for 50 to 60 minutes, until a knife inserted in center comes out clean.

Serves 6.

PEANUT BUTTER & JAM BARS

ANGELA MURPHY
TEMPE, AZ

Everyone's favorite flavors!

Combine cookie mix, oil, water and egg; stir into a soft dough. Add chips and mix well. Press dough into a lightly greased 13"x9" baking pan. Bake at 350 degrees for 15 to 18 minutes, until edges are light golden. Cool completely, about 30 minutes. Stir frosting, milk and peanut butter together until well blended. Spread over baked crust. Drop jam by teaspoonfuls over frosting mixture; swirl jam with a knife tip to create a marbled design. Refrigerate for 20 minutes, or until set. Slice into bars.

Makes about 3 dozen.

17-1/2 oz. pkg. peanut butter cookie mix

3 T. oil

1 T. water

1 egg, beaten

1/2 c. peanut butter chips

16-oz. container vanilla frosting

1 T. milk

1/4 c. creamy peanut butter

1/4 c. strawberry jam

CRANBERRY MOUSSE

CHERYL WESTFALL
SURPRISE, AZ

A requested recipe by family members for all holiday gatherings!

In a saucepan over medium heat, heat cranberry juice to boiling. Add gelatin mix; stir until dissolved. Remove from heat; stir in cranberry sauce. Cover and chill until mixture is thickened. In a bowl, beat cream with an electric mixer on high speed until soft peaks form. Fold whipped cream into gelatin mixture; spoon into a glass bowl or individual dessert dishes. Cover and chill until firm. Garnish with additional whipped cream, if desired.

Serves 8.

1 c. cranberry juice cocktail

3-oz. pkg. raspberry gelatin mix

15-oz. can whole-berry cranberry sauce

1 c. heavy cream, whipped

Optional: additional whipped cream

SLOW-COOKER APPLE CAKE

MARY GARCIA
PHOENIX, AZ

So good during the fall season and perfectly paired with hot apple cider on a cold morning!

2 c. biscuit baking mix
2/3 c. applesauce
1/4 c. milk
2 T. sugar
2 T. butter, softened
2 apples, peeled, cored and diced
1/2 c. finely chopped pecans
1 t. cinnamon
1 t. vanilla extract
1 egg, lightly beaten

In a large bowl, combine all ingredients; mix well. Spoon batter into a lightly greased slow cooker; Cover and cook on high setting for 2-1/2 to 3 hours, until a toothpick inserted in the center of cake tests clean. Uncover and remove crock to a wire rack to cool. Loosen sides of cake with a thin spatula; remove cake and slice to serve.

Serves 8.

FORGOTTEN COOKIES

WENDY MCDONALD
GLENDALE, AZ

Our family has been enjoying these flourless cookies for over ten years. I think you'll love them too!

2 egg whites, room temperature
3/4 c. sugar
1/8 t. salt
1 t. vanilla extract
1 c. mini semi-sweet chocolate chips
Optional: 1 c. chopped pecans

Preheat oven to 350 degrees. Beat egg whites with an electric mixer on high speed until foamy. Gradually add sugar, beating until stiff peaks form. Stir in remaining ingredients. Drop by teaspoonfuls onto ungreased aluminum foil-lined baking sheets. Place baking sheets in oven; immediately turn oven off and allow to cool. Leave cookies in closed oven overnight.

Makes about 4 dozen.

NUTMEG FEATHER CAKE

FAYE MAYBERRY
SAINT DAVID, AZ

This recipe was discovered in a vintage cookbook dated 1952. I was instantly intrigued with it because I like nutmeg and have never come upon a strictly nutmeg-flavored cake. We top warm servings with a pat of butter and they are heavenly!

Blend together shortening and sugar. Add eggs; beat well. Whisk together flour, salt, baking powder, baking soda and nutmeg; set aside. In a separate small bowl, combine buttermilk and vanilla. Add flour mixture to shortening mixture alternately with buttermilk mixture. Spread in a greased, wax paper-lined 13"x9" baking pan. Bake at 350 degrees for 25 to 30 minutes, or until cake is golden and tests done.

Serves 8 to 10.

1/4 c. butter, softened
1/4 c. shortening
1-1/2 c. sugar
3 eggs, beaten
2 c. all-purpose flour
1/4 t. salt
1 t. baking powder
1 t. baking soda
2 t. nutmeg
1 c. buttermilk
1/2 t. vanilla extract

DATE-NUT ROLL

MARY COKER
APACHE JUNCTION, AZ

My mother used to make this recipe. So easy and delicious...rich and wonderful! Very good served with a cup of coffee or tea.

Mix graham cracker crumbs, pecans and dates in a large bowl; set aside. In the top of a double boiler over hot water, melt marshmallows in milk; add to crumb mixture and mix well. Spoon mixture onto wax paper and form into a long roll with your hands. Wrap and chill. To serve, slice in 1/4-inch slices. Top with whipped cream, if desired.

Makes 12 servings.

25 graham crackers, crushed
4 c. chopped pecans
4 c. chopped dates
25 large marshmallows
1/2 c. milk
Optional: whipped cream

BETTE'S CHOCOLATE & PEPPERMINT ROLL

**BEV FISHER
MESA, AZ**

When I was in grade school, every Christmas my mother made this dessert to take to her women's club meeting. It was the most delicious thing I had ever tasted!

1 c. whipping cream
1 t. vanilla extract
2 T. powdered sugar
9-oz. pkg. plain chocolate wafers
1 c. peppermint candy, coarsely crushed

In a large bowl, beat cream, vanilla and sugar with an electric mixer on high speed until stiff peaks form. Spread a little whipped cream on both sides of each wafer. Stack wafers to form a long roll; place roll on its side on a serving plate. Spread remaining whipped cream over top and sides of roll; sprinkle with crushed candy. Wrap lightly with plastic wrap and freeze for 4 hours to overnight. Just before serving, slice on the diagonal to show stripes of cream and chocolate.

Makes 10 to 12 servings.

JOSHUA'S BUTTERSCOTCH CAKE

**LINDA SMITH
FOUNTAIN HILLS, AZ**

This is my son's favorite cake and it is so easy to make. Serve as either a morning coffee cake or a dinner dessert. Needs no icing and is very moist. What more could you want?

18-1/2 oz. pkg. yellow cake mix
4 3-1/4 oz. cups butterscotch pudding
2 eggs, beaten
6-oz. pkg. butterscotch chips
1/3 c. sugar

In a large bowl, combine cake mix, pudding and eggs; beat until well mixed. Pour batter into a greased 13"x9" baking pan. Sprinkle butterscotch chips and sugar over batter and press in. Bake at 350 degrees for 30 to 35 minutes; do not overbake.

Makes 12 servings.

FRUIT DUMP CAKE

**KATHY KEHRING
SCOTTSDALE, AZ**

A scrumptious quick & easy dessert that's always a winner at family get-togethers and potlucks.

Spray a 5-quart slow cooker with non-stick vegetable spray. Layer undrained pineapple, undrained pears and cranberries. Sprinkle with brown sugar, ginger and dry cake mix. Arrange butter on top. Cover and cook on low setting for 3 to 4 hours, until a toothpick inserted in center comes out clean. To serve, scoop into dessert bowls. Serve warm, topped with ice cream or whipped cream, if desired.

Makes 12 servings.

15-oz. can crushed
  pineapple
15-oz. can sliced pears
12-oz. pkg. fresh
  cranberries
1/2 c. brown sugar,
  packed
1 t. ground ginger
18-1/2 oz. pkg. yellow
  cake mix
1/2 c. butter, sliced
Optional: vanilla ice
  cream or whipped
  cream

BETH'S QUICK & EASY FRUIT COBBLER

**CYNTHIA DODGE
QUEEN CREEK, AZ**

One of my best friends gave me this super-quick recipe over 25 years ago. It had been in her family for years before that. We love it too!

In a bowl, mix together flour, sugar, milk and margarine. Spoon batter into a greased 8"x8" glass baking pan. Add pie filling over batter by spoonfuls. Bake at 350 degrees for 45 to 50 minutes, until golden. Serve warm, garnished as desired.

Serves 4 to 6.

1 c. all-purpose flour
1 c. sugar
1 c. milk
1/2 c. margarine, melted
21-oz. can favorite fruit
  pie filling
Garnish: vanilla ice
  cream or whipped
  topping

HOOSIER CAKE

SHERRY SHEEHAN
PHOENIX, AZ

This recipe was handed down on my father's side of the family by my favorite aunt, Aunt Jeanette. She regularly brought this cake to family reunions, and it disappeared almost as quickly as it appeared.

1-1/2 c. hot water
1 c. quick-cooking oats, uncooked
1 c. light brown sugar, packed
1 c. sugar
1 t. vanilla extract
2 eggs
1/2 c. shortening
1-1/2 c. all-purpose flour
1 t. salt
1 t. baking soda
1 t. cinnamon
1 c. raisins

COCONUT-PECAN ICING
1/2 c. butter
1 c. brown sugar, packed
12-oz. can evaporated milk
1 t. vanilla extract
2 c. shredded coconut
1 c. chopped pecans

In a bowl, combine water and oats; set aside. In another bowl, combine sugars, vanilla, eggs and shortening. Mix well. Stir in oat mixture. Add remaining ingredients to oat mixture; stir to blend well. Spoon batter into a greased 13"x9" baking pan. Bake at 350 degrees for 35 to 40 minutes, until a toothpick inserted in the center tests clean. Remove from oven and cool; spread with Coconut-Pecan Frosting.

Serves 12 to 15.

Coconut-Pecan Icing:
In a saucepan over medium heat, combine butter, brown sugar and milk. Bring to a boil and cook, stirring constantly, until thickened. Remove from heat; stir in vanilla, coconut and pecans.

POPCORN CAKE

MELISSA CURRIE
PHOENIX, AZ

When I taught third grade, my students would enjoy helping make this fun popcorn cake in the morning, to enjoy in the afternoon before the bell rang to go home. Get ready for ooohs and aahs!

Use 2 tablespoons butter to coat a smooth tube pan. Sprinkle a handful of plain candies in bottom of pan and set aside. In a very large bowl, combine popcorn, remaining plain candies, peanut candies and peanuts. In a saucepan over medium heat, melt remaining butter and marshmallows. Stir until smooth; pour over popcorn mixture and mix well. Pack mixture tightly into tube pan; cover and refrigerate at least 1-1/2 hours. Run a knife around edge and center of pan. Invert onto a plate; slice like a cake.

Makes 8 to 10 servings.

1/2 c. plus
2 T. butter, divided
16-oz. pkg. plain candy-coated chocolates, divided
6 c. lightly salted popcorn
16-oz. pkg. peanut candy-coated chocolates
16-oz. jar dry-roasted peanuts
16-oz. pkg. marshmallows

KITCHEN TIP

When recipes call for room-temperature ingredients, it's important to follow these directions. (Cold butter will not cream and cold eggs can curdle the batter.) To quickly bring eggs to room temperature, place them in a bowl under running, warm tap water for a few minutes.

INDEX

Mains

Salads

INDEX continued

U.S. to METRIC RECIPE EQUIVALENTS

Volume Measurements

¼ teaspoon...................... 1 mL
½ teaspoon...................... 2 mL
1 teaspoon .... 5 mL
1 tablespoon = 3 teaspoons...... 15 mL
2 tablespoons = 1 fluid ounce .... 30 mL
¼ cup.......................... 60 mL
⅓ cup.......................... 75 mL
½ cup = 4 fluid ounces.......... 125 mL
1 cup = 8 fluid ounces .... 250 mL
2 cups = 1 pint = 16 fluid ounces 500 mL
4 cups = 1 quart .... 1 L

Weights

1 ounce .... 30 g
4 ounces .... 120 g
8 ounces .... 225 g
16 ounces = 1 pound .... 450 g

Baking Pan Sizes

Square
8x8x2 inches .... 2 L = 20x20x5 cm
9x9x2 inches ...... 2.5 L = 23x23x5 cm

Rectangular
13x9x2 inches ..... 3.5 L = 33x23x5 cm

Loaf
9x5x3 inches .... 2 L = 23x13x7 cm

Round
8x1½ inches .... 1.2 L = 20x4 cm
9x1½ inches .... 1.5 L = 23x4 cm

Recipe Abbreviations

t. = teaspoon......... ltr. = liter
T. = tablespoon........ oz. = ounce
c. = cup............... lb. = pound
pt. = pint...............doz. = dozen
qt. = quart.......... ....pkg. = package
gal. = gallon............env. = envelope

Oven Temperatures

300° F...............150° C
325° F...............160° C
350° F...............180° C
375° F...............190° C
400° F...............200° C
450° F...............230° C

Kitchen Measurements

A pinch = ⅛ tablespoon
1 fluid ounce = 2 tablespoons
3 teaspoons = 1 tablespoon
4 fluid ounces = ½ cup
2 tablespoons = ⅛ cup
8 fluid ounces = 1 cup
4 tablespoons = ¼ cup
16 fluid ounces = 1 pint
8 tablespoons = ½ cup
32 fluid ounces = 1 quart
16 tablespoons = 1 cup
16 ounces net weight = 1 pound
2 cups = 1 pint
4 cups = 1 quart
4 quarts = 1 gallon

Send us your favorite recipe

and the memory that makes it special for you!*

If we select your recipe for a brand-new **Gooseberry Patch** cookbook, your name will appear right along with it...and you'll receive a FREE copy of the book!

Submit your recipe on our website at

www.gooseberrypatch.com/sharearecipe

*Please include the number of servings and all other necessary information.

Have a taste for more?

Visit www.gooseberrypatch.com to join our Circle of Friends!

• Free recipes, tips and ideas plus a complete cookbook index
• Get mouthwatering recipes and special email offers delivered to your inbox.

You'll also love these cookbooks from **Gooseberry Patch**!

A Year Of Holidays
Christmas for Sharing
Classic Church Potlucks
Farmhouse Kitchen
Our Best Cast-Iron Cooking Recipes
Our Best Recipes from Grandma's Cookie Jar
Quick & Easy Recipes with Help
Shortcuts to Grandma's Best Recipes
Slow Cookers, Casseroles & Skillets
Welcome Autumn

www.gooseberrypatch.com